The Creative
Dreamer

MICHAEL BEAM

The Creative Dreamer

REVISED

Using Your Dreams to Unlock Your Creativity

by Veronica Tonay, Ph.D.

CELESTIAL ARTS
Berkeley | Toronto

CA

Celestial Arts
P.O. Box 7123
Berkeley, CA 94707

Distributed in Australia by Simon and Schuster; in Canada by Publishers Group West; in New Zealand by Tandem Press; in South Africa by Real Books; and in the United Kingdom and Europe by Airlift Books

Cover and text design by Chloe Rawlins
Cover illustration by Jing Jing/Getty Images
Illustrated by Mike Gray

Library of Congress Cataloging-in-Publication Data
Tonay, Veronica.
   The creative dreamer, revised : using your dreams to unlock your creativity /
   By Veronica Tonay.
     ISBN 13: 978-1-58761-268-8 (pbk.)
     ISBN 10: 1-58761-268-2 (pbk.)
     1. Dreams. 2. Creative ability. I. Title.
   BF1091.T66 1995
     154.6'3—dc20   95-18405
CIP

Printed in China

1 2 3 4 5 6 7 8 9 10 — 10 09 08 07 06

≋ Contents ≋

≋ Acknowledgments ≋

I WOULD LIKE TO THANK my thirty undergraduate research assistants at the University of California at Santa Cruz, especially: Jennifer Barry, Jonathan Benak, Melissa Bow, Kaitlin Bowman, Sharon Corbett, Lisa Henkemeyer, Jon Reynolds, Leslie Smith, and Karen Sutton. Their tireless work coding dream series enabled me to complete some of the most time-intensive research I could have chosen and formed the foundation for this book. I would also like to acknowledge the contribution of the hundreds of participants in my research, who gave freely of their most personal dreams.

The work of psychologist Carl Jung and his followers, and of Drs. Calvin S. Hall and Frank Barron most inspired this book. It was born at the University of California at Berkeley, where Dr. Gerald Mendelsohn taught me to strive for perfection and accept my best, to persevere in the face of personal crisis, and to acquire a taste for caramel mints. I thank him, and other Cal mentors, Drs. Oliver John and Mac Runyan, for supporting me as a creative psychologist who dreams. At the University of California at Santa Cruz, I thank Dr. William Domhoff for encouraging my work with dreams. I am also grateful to my brother, Joe, and late parents, who engendered in me a commitment to the truth, to compassion, and to helping others.

After the first printing of *The Creative Dreamer*, many readers wrote to me to let me know how the book helped them to acknowledge and express their creativity, and even, in some cases, to change their lives. I am honored by those notes and grateful to readers for sharing their thoughts, experiences, and dreams with me. I can be reached through my website, www.drtonay.com, and I will respond if you write!

Many psychotherapy clients, students, and dream group participants revealed their inner lives to me over the past ten years by sharing their dreams and giving me permission to discuss them here. Their brave vulnerability in doing so was a gift, and I thank them.

My own, small creative community is a solace and a gentle spur. Rewriting this book, I am again reminded of how important each individual person can be in the life of someone who creates. Thank you, my friends! Over the past ten years, I lost Frank Barron and Kay Kelly, two nourishing, magical, and wise friends. Giving voice to my own creative spirit during times of loss and change led new worlds to present themselves. Steven is one of those worlds, giving of himself by standing with me, holding my candle in the dark, making me laugh, and reminding me of who I am.

Finally, I want to thank Lily, my kind, lovely, and brilliant editor, for her encouragement and sage advice. I am grateful to her and to everyone at Celestial Arts for enthusiastically giving me the opportunity to reach out again.

Without all of these people, this book wouldn't be. Thank you all.

≈≈ Preface ≈≈

I AM ONE WHO IS captivated by dreams. How did I get here, writing these words you are now reading? When I was nineteen and still shivering from adolescence, I decided to seek therapy. I was in college, majoring in dance, which represented freedom and life to me, when I contracted chronic tendonitis in my knee. I was forced to give up dancing. With hardly a pause and no display of grief, I decided to become an English literature teacher, giving up my ideas of becoming a dancer for something more "practical."

My new psychologist listened thoughtfully to my tale. She asked about what kind of dreams I had been having. I had always wondered what part of myself dreams came from and what, if anything, they meant for me to know. I had kept a dream journal since I was thirteen, the age at which most girls (including me) turn inward and outward simultaneously, often ripping ourselves nearly in half in the process, before mending the rip to scar and grow again.

I stared back at her, surprised to realize: "I haven't remembered a dream in ages."

She nodded, slowly. "That makes sense."

It didn't to me.

"You have lost your dreams," she said.

So began the path of my sometimes shaggy education. As a psychologist (who could resist such a provocative and mysterious initiation? I abandoned literature at once!), I have heard or read some

25,000 dreams from people all over the world, people of various ages and life experiences and backgrounds. This book is based in part on research I performed, using about 3,000 dreams from more than 200 generous people, for my master's and doctoral degrees at the University of California at Berkeley: research attempting to connect dreaming with personality and, more specifically, with creativity. *The Creative Dreamer* is also enriched by the dreams and experiences of my many students at the University of California, my dream group and workshop participants, and my psychotherapy clients, whose contributions I honor and am deeply grateful for.

I blend many perspectives in my work with dreams. Not every dream lends itself to interpretation, and not all dreams can be interpreted from a single point of view. The first part of this book also relies upon the original work of psychologists Calvin S. Hall and Robert Van de Castle, who developed a method for researching the content of dreams.[1] They found that dreams reflect our waking-life conceptions of the world, our society, and ourselves.

In my own work researching dreams, I found that most theories of dreaming (including the neurobiological "explanations" of dreams) can be integrated. In the first part of *The Creative Dreamer*, I incorporated the dream models of Jung, Freud, Hall, Perls, and Boss to the extent that their theories have been supported by research. The first part of the book will most interest those who like numbers, facts, and categories.

It is unwise to rely only upon one's intellect, however: meaning may easily be misplaced along the way. And so the rest of the book becomes more Jungian, as we journey into the heart of the psyche's dark forest, encountering feelings and recurrent themes.

Carl Gustav Jung, a Swiss physician who studied psychoanalysis and then moved on to develop his own theory of personality, believed that our dreams portray in images our individual feelings and thoughts. Those psychologists who built upon his theory all value dreams as potential treasure chests of self-understanding. We dream about that within us which is unknown, and by attending to our dreams, we are awakened to our real selves. Fantasy, daydreaming, artistic expression, and dreams all hold keys to our own inner depths.

It is impossible to treat dreams completely and with the depth they demand in a volume of this size. I attempted to maintain the integrity of the various models presented here, with the understanding that so much more could always be written. I hope this book will be useful to everyone, and to that end, notes are included for those who are hungry for more. There, you will find additional resources for your inner journey.

The pendulum swings for us all from waking to sleep, dark to light, back and forth, night after night, dream after dream. As fascinating and full of wonder as those dreams are, the dreamers of dreams are even more so. That is why this is not so much a book of dreams as a book of dreamers—dreamers who create worlds every night, and like to do so while awake, too. In writing this book, I wish to encourage creative people to take an honest look inward, unmask their own unique selves, give back to the world their creative gifts, and feel renewed and less alone in the process. May this book be a friendly companion to you as you walk upon your creative path.

Welcome, and good morning!

≋ Introduction ≋

WE HAVE LOST OUR WAY. Between the lines of the newspaper and the billboards along the freeway, over the buzz of our machines and the drone of the newscasters, we have forgotten our dreams. What we used to turn to even a hundred years ago as a source of meaning, inspiration, and magical feeling, many of us now regard as irrelevant bits of brain chatter. Some even dismiss dreams as silly, bizarre, and irrational.

But our dreams are irrational the way our feelings are irrational, and both are important to a creative life. As Freud observed, "Dreams are often most profound when they seem most crazy." Dreams provide an unexpected gift: a glimpse into our own creative process every morning.

The Creative Dreamer is meant for all of us. Although we may think of musicians, writers, painters, and so on as being creative, creative people exist in many fields, including science, business, education, and public service.

Whether or not you think of yourself as creative, you are. Creativity is defined as bringing something new and valuable into existence. Each night, each one of us creates when we dream. We shape our dream worlds in ways that are imaginative and fresh. You are probably reading this book because you believe your dreams mean something (which they do) and can help you to move beyond your creative blocks to find new ways to express yourself in the world.

Henry David Thoreau observed, "Dream.
of our characters." For me, dreams really are a touchstone. They
remind me of aspects of myself I have forgotten and of situations
and feelings I need to attend to. They keep me honest and humble
by gently (sometimes, not so gently!) prodding me when I am overwhelmed with unrealistic goals or am being overly harsh with
myself. I find them to be windows into the lives and feelings of the
clients with whom I work in my psychotherapy practice.

Aside from the personal inspiration dreams provide (more on
that in chapter 4), dreams are essential not only because they can
teach us about ourselves, but also because they reflect what is going
on under the surface of our culture: common themes that concern,
frighten, enrapture, or uplift us—the psychic undercurrents of
our world. Dreams mirror what is unknown and unexpressed in
all of us. For example, the large number of women who consistently
dream of being victims of violence reflects the appalling rate of
actual violence against women in the waking world and in today's
films and literature. Some researchers are noticing how much more
frequently religious themes occur in the dreams of contemporary
Western people than in our culture's past. We do seem to be a spir-
itually lost and seeking society, a state of being that is now often
represented in our dream life. As prominent creativity researcher
Frank Barron noted, it is no accident that the recent prevalence of
the "end of the world" theme in creative works also surfaces in our
dreams. A collection of dreams about the end of the world has even
been published. Whether the presence of this imagery in Western
dreams presages an actual cataclysmic event or transformation, or

simply illustrates our largely unconscious concern about the possibility of the world's ending, only time will tell.

We all have blind spots, and as a species, we share some of them: humans have the potential to do terrible things to one another (things like genocide, torture, or other forms of abuse), and also to be extraordinarily generous, kind, and wise. We each have the potential to behave in all of these ways under certain conditions.

The capacity for this kind of extreme behavior is hard for most of us to recognize within ourselves; and since it is unconscious, it can be dangerous. The unrecognized potential for extreme aggression, for instance, might explain why humans' dreams are typically quite violent (see chapter 1). The flourishing of culture and society rests on the degree to which we can distinguish our own feelings and motives from those of other groups. Is it *really* that group *x* or nation *y* is greedy and territorial, or are those qualities that our own society is not addressing within itself? Are we, as individuals, greedy and territorial?

Once we recognize that we have the capacity to express these qualities and begin to address them within ourselves, the intensity of our anger at the "other" decreases and we are better able to evaluate and act on the truth of the situation. The better we know ourselves, as individuals and as societies, the less likely we are to harm other people by intentionally or unintentionally accusing them of things we have not yet addressed in ourselves.

If we collectively continue to run from feelings and from the irrational, including the world of dreams, we will find ourselves face to face with what we fear and in an even more perilous state than we now find ourselves. Whenever we create—whether as artists, scientists, teachers, gardeners, or dreamers—we foreshadow the future by being sensitive to, interpreting, and expressing what goes unexpressed in the world. When creating something new, we are more in touch with unconscious material than other people are (as we will see in chapters 3 and 5). Our work becomes a mirror, held up to the world, which reflects back upon us and others what is so difficult for us to face—the horror and heaven of being human.

How to Use This Book

The Creative Dreamer offers you a way to use your own dreams to enhance your self-understanding and your creative work. It presents an eclectic view of dream interpretation, based on both research and theory. In part I, you will discover how people's dreams are similar all over the world, what makes men's and women's dreams different, and how typical or unique your own dreams are. You will then explore the qualities of people who live extraordinarily creative lives, including their dreams. In part II, you will mine the rich earth of your dream landscapes, uncovering themes and elements—such as children and loss—that often appear in dreams of those who create, and will learn how those elements can help you express your creativity. In part III you will enter the deepest territory, traveling an inner road to discover how these dream themes reflect feelings and aspects of yourself of which you may not be aware. You will find how unexpressed emotions can inhibit and even sabotage you, and will learn keys to unlock your creativity in the face of sometimes powerful opposition from without and within.

Various exercises are sprinkled throughout the book. These will enable you to assess your own creativity, creative dreaming, and creative potential; use your unique dream themes to interpret your own dreams; work through your creative blocks; and form a creative community.

Finally, each chapter closes with a scene that stretches the imagination: an "exercise" that keeps creativity flowing. As you move through the book, these passages will slowly lead you into the psyche's inner dark woods and back out again, finding and bringing with you the treasure of your own creative spring. As you read these lines, relax and visualize yourself within the images, as if you were in a dream.

Keeping a Dream Journal

Because we have no conscious control over our dreams, they can provide snapshots of the condition of our own souls. Your dreams will not hide you from yourself, no matter how unpleasant or flattering the view, as long as you keep looking. A dream journal gives you a record of yourself observing yourself. It says things about you that you might not otherwise know until much time has passed: your dreams can help you see parts of yourself you might ordinarily miss—parts that, if recognized and welcomed, can help you become more like yourself and less like everyone else.

If you don't already, keep a dream journal as you journey through this book. *The Creative Dreamer* offers a number of exercises for you to use to explore your own dream life. Many of these exercises invite you to reflect upon your own dreams in order to better know yourself and your creative process. If you have not been writing down your dreams, I encourage you to begin tonight.

≈ Introduction to the Revised Edition ≈

WELCOME TO THE REVISED EDITION of *The Creative Dreamer*! As a psychologist in private practice, a university teacher, a workshop leader, and, most recently, a dream expert on the Discovery Health channel's television program *Dream Decoders*, I have learned so much over the past ten years. I am happy to have the opportunity to enrich this, my first book, with wisdom gained from experiences with so many more creative dreams and dreamers.

In this edition, I added exercises on how to use your dreams to enhance creativity. These were refined as I led dream groups and workshops all over the world. Meeting so many dreamers and creative people, I am reminded that so many of us are searching for ways to become more whole, and to share with others more of who and what we are. As time passes, I realize that although dreams remain ephemeral and mysterious, their pure reflection of what we value, whom we love, and how we can best give, is pure gold in our modern landscape of quick fixes and superficial insights.

Once again, I learned that befriending your dreams and allowing them to help you in your creative life is not about dissecting images frozen in the frame of your memory. Dreams are a living part of you, and your understanding of them is enriched in the same way you learn more about your friends: through paying attention to, listening, and honoring them. In return, your dreams greet you with yourself each morning, reminding you of your location, your path, and all of the creative wonders within you.

Santa Cruz, California, October, 2005

Part I

Dreams and
Dream Makers:
Across the Meadow

We are the music makers,
We are the dreamers of dreams,
Wandering by lone sea-breakers,
And sitting by desolate streams—
World-losers and world-forsakers,
On whom the pale moon gleams,
Yet we are the movers and shakers
Of the world for ever, it seems.

—Arthur O'Shaughnessy, from *Ode*[2]

Chapter 1

What Are Dreams Like?

WE ARE ALL DREAMERS OF DREAMS. Populated with creatures and people who do and say uncanny things, our dreams unsettle us and leave us wondering at their meaning. Because dreams originate inside of us, they can tell us a lot about ourselves, and although we may find our dreams strange because they do not speak as we do, dreams do not disguise. They show us a reality based in images, not on words—much like the reality we knew before we could speak. But what can we do with what we see there? There are no maps to help us negotiate our dreamscapes.

Suppose you had the following dream:

> An acquaintance I knew ran by me and a group, scream-ing and holding her head. "Get me out! I need to leave! Get me out of here!" She ran into the woods. We decided we had to help her, so we all ran after her, but we came

to the edge of the sea. She had gone to the other side and the only way we could get there was to cross the water. We got in and started inching across using these handles that were attached to a wall. We moved across slowly, hand by hand, as if we were children in a beginning swimming class, scared of the water. The water started swelling and violently moving—we were scared of drowning. I suddenly grew very impatient. The people in front of me were going too slow. I began to move very fast, passing them up, trying to keep my head above the waves since I had to let go of the handles to pass them.

I got to the other side, and when I got out (I was in a place that looked like the Old City of Jerusalem), everything was made of stone. I walked and eventually came to a doctor's office. I asked about Sharon, the woman who had run by us, screaming. They said the doctor was seeing her and I should wait. I looked around and saw a little brown dog on a chair. It was lying on its back and its whole front side, neck to abdomen, was cut open, the skin pulled back and its organs sat neatly inside. I distinctly remember its two front paws, they were bent and playing with its insides. I reached over and pulled out the heart. It was wrapped in Saran Wrap and it was beating. . . I bought something to eat. People kept telling me how dangerous and unclean it was for me to eat food while I was holding this beating heart. I began a very intricate eating pattern, the food and the heart were rolling on my fingers, and I had to move my hands to keep them from falling or touching.

It began to get dark and I realized I needed to get back. I began running, clutching my food and the heart tightly. I didn't know how to get back. An old woman with a young son started running next to me. We were all hunched over, legs bent, running as if we were ducking from something. We began to race each other. I stopped suddenly. A long, empty stone road was before me. No people, just darkness and moonlight. I saw, way in the distance, Leah, a woman I'd worked with for two weeks on an archeological dig. She was squatting on the road, and as I looked at her, she pointed her finger in the direction I should go and a glowing green light indicated the distance. It grew out of her finger like those light saber swords from *Star Wars*.

If this were your dream, what would you make of it? The dreamer of this elaborate dream is Giselle, a dancer-choreographer.[3] Before reading on, you might want to write down your impressions of her dream. Consider, using your own intuition, what the dream might be saying about Giselle's life, strengths, conflicts, and fears. At the end of this book, you will have an opportunity to revisit Giselle's dream to see what you have learned by reading *The Creative Dreamer*. For now, speculate wildly as you consider possible connections between the dream and Giselle's creative expression.

When we dream, we transform our longings and our fears into strangely familiar images and landscapes. When we create in the waking world, we often portray our pasts, our futures, our presents—sometimes metaphorically, sometimes literally. So it is with our dreams: we fall into a secret place at bedtime and make more than a movie, more than an illustrated short story, and more than a poem.

When we wake, we wonder whether these creations of ours are anything like anyone else's. Are we crazy to be dreaming like this?

What kinds of dreams do our neighbors and friends have? People from other places? Famous people? Before we explore how we can use our dreams to help us, we will need to know what kinds of things make our dreams similar to everyone else's. Then we can see what makes our own dreams creative and unique.

Dreaming across Cultures

In the 1930s, anthropologist Lauriston Sharp ventured to Australia and collected 140 dreams from forty-three members of the Yir Yoront, an Australian aboriginal culture.[4] The American psychologists who later independently analyzed these dreams (David Schneider and Calvin S. Hall) concluded that the elements of Yir Yoronts' and Americans' dreams are more similar than different.

Not only are the dreams of the Yir Yoront and of people all over the U.S. similar, so too are the dreams of people all over the globe. Dreamers in Mexico, Peru, India, the Netherlands, Switzerland, Canada, Argentina, Japan; dreamers of the Hopi, Ifaluk, Alor, Tinguian, Skolt, Baija, Kuatiutl, and Navaho tribes; the Mehinaku dreamers in the central Brazilian Amazon rainforest; the Zapatecs in Southern Mexico; and the Gusii, Kipsigis, and Logoli of East Africa all have the same kinds of dreams. Even the most isolated of these groups contributed dreams for study long before industrialized societies moved in.[5]

How then are all human dreams similar?

• All over the world, we dream most often of groups of people we know.

- Those dream people are often physically aggressive—chasing, confining, or attacking us or other dream characters.

- Bad things happen to us in dreams more often than do good things. Our dream characters suffer misfortunes like natural disasters, illness, amnesia, broken or lost things, or lost people.

So a typical human dream contains a group of people the dreamer knows who aggressively interact with each other and the dreamer. Also, somewhere within the dream, someone experiences a misfortune. It would seem that our dreamlands are far from ideal, but we should be cautious in judging and interpreting our dreams. Far from being symptomatic of some underlying disorder, a certain degree of aggression and misfortune come with the dreaming territory.

We all share certain basic human experiences. We are curious, questing, and fragile beings, frightened by vast emptiness and longing for sustenance and warmth. We are tenacious, we hope, and we seek meaning. We are born; we learn and grow; we become attracted to others and start families; we work; we age; we die. And we all dream. And whether or not we are creative, our dreams are in many ways variations on the same dream. The elements of this common dream cannot, by themselves, tell us much about our own personalities and conflicts. But if we know what kinds of dream elements can be explained by universal principles, we can avoid "overinterpreting" and identify and focus on what is unique in our dreams.

Men's and Women's Dreams

Some aspects of our dreams are shared with other members of our sex.[6] As in the cross-cultural findings on dreams, there are surprisingly few differences between men's and women's dreams. It will be helpful to know how they do compare, though, so you can tell how typical of your sex your own dreams are. If you find your dream elements are not very similar to the ones described for your sex, never fear: people who create tend to be more psychologically *androgynous* than average, which means they manifest both typically masculine and feminine personality traits.

Psychologists and anthropologists found, after performing dream studies all over the world, that:

WOMEN	MEN
Dream equally of men and women	Dream more often of men
Dream more often of familiar people	Dream more often of strangers
Dream of themselves as victims of another's aggression more often than do men	Have more aggression (usually physical) in their dreams than do women, and are more often the initiators of aggression
Have about the same number of friendly and aggressive dream encounters	Have aggressive dream encounters more often than friendly ones

Those who performed much of this research found that, in American culture, our dreams reflect our waking experience remarkably well. American men's dream lives are full of men with whom they are competing and fighting because in their waking lives, men do compete; they often seem to be "fighting" their way to the top. American women, on the other hand, tend to be more interpersonally oriented than are men, and their dreams have lots of familiar, friendly people in them. In the waking world, women are more often the victims of attack than the initiators of attacks. It is no surprise, then, that women dream of being victims of verbal and physical attacks more often than they do of being the instigators of those attacks.

Most of these male/female patterns in dreaming are consistent across cultures and also across time. The women's movement brought some dreaming changes: I found that American women in 1990 were more assertive in their dreams (and, perhaps, in their lives) than were women in 1950. Otherwise, the dream elements of women (and men) have remained largely the same.[7]

In anyone's dreams, then, there will be plenty of aggression, more groups than individuals, more misfortune than good fortune. In women's dreams, there will also be more victimization, and more familiar people. In men's dreams, there will be more strangers, and more aggression than friendliness.

So, if you often dream of yourself being anxious and afraid in the midst of a group of people, and then something bad happens to you, that probably has less to do with who you are than it does with your being human. The energy spent interpreting those elements of your dreams as if they were indicative of deep-seated conflict might be better used by exploring your most creative dreams, whose imagery and landscape are unique. Of course, you may still find conflict there, but at least you will have avoided overinterpreting common dream material.

□ ～ □ ～ □ ～ □ ～ □ ～ □ ～ □ ～ □ ～ □ ～ □

Exercise: Man or Woman?

Knowing what you now know about the differences between men's and women's dreams, see whether you can tell if this dreamer, "Chris," is a man or a woman:

> DREAM ONE: I was at an awards presentation with Rita [familiar woman]. An admiral [unfamiliar man] came up to me and gave me a ring that had a little steel ball in it. If you shook the ring, the little steel ball would roll around and make a chiming sound. The admiral asked me to join the Navy.

> DREAM TWO: Mark [familiar man] and I are sitting on a couch...Mark father [familiar] was down the hall and then comes in and pulls me away. Next, I'm with Rita [familiar woman], who's encouraging me to buy some kind of electrical device.

> DREAM THREE: I feel lost. My brother, Richard, is there. He tells me I don't have the right books and helps me to get the right ones. An old friend, Denise [familiar woman], is also there, and helps me to get what I need.

> DREAM FOUR: I'm in some kind of rickety theater. Phil Donahue [talk show host] is backstage. He is holding a baby [one of my cousins, a girl] who is crying. I ran in there because a group of some men [strangers] are trying to beat me up. I hold the baby and rock it to sleep. I follow Mr. Donahue to his house, but he doesn't want me to...The guys find me. I ask them who they are...They beat me up and leave. I go to Donahue's house. He says I can stay and he will help me.

Now, for each dream, mark the number of times you observe the following (D = the dreamer):

Dream Number

1	2	3	4	Total	
___	___	___	___	___	1) Someone (not D) is aggressive*
___	___	___	___	___	2) D is aggressive
___	___	___	___	___	3) Someone (not D) is victimized**
___	___	___	___	___	4) D is victimized
___	___	___	___	___	5) Someone is friendly***
___	___	___	___	___	6) Number of males
___	___	___	___	___	7) Number of females
___	___	___	___	___	8) Number of people D knows
___	___	___	___	___	9) Number of strangers

* "Aggressive" means verbally yelling at or insulting another; thinking aggressive thoughts; physically confining, chasing, stealing from, coercing, or hurting another; or attempting to do so. It can also be done to the self.
** "Victimized" means the character is the focus of aggression.
*** "Friendly" means one character visits another; gives another something; invites another somewhere; says a kind thing to, helps, or thinks positive thoughts about another; or is physically—not sexually—affectionate to another. Friendliness does not mean simply associating with another. It can also be expressed toward the self.

Once you have added up the numbers for each dream (1–4) for all items (1–9), use those totals and check the table to see whether or not Chris's dreams are more likely a woman's or a man's:

WOMAN	MAN
Item 4 is greater than item 2	Item 4 is less than item 2
Item 1 is equal to or less than item 5	Item 1 is greater than item 5
Item 6 is about equal to item 7	Item 6 is greater than item 7
Item 8 is greater than item 9	Item 8 is less than item 9

DREAM ONE

Two friendly interactions (D is given a
    gift and is invited to join the Navy)
One male character (Admiral)
One female (Rita)
One familiar person (Rita)
One stranger (Admiral)

DREAM TWO

Two men (Mark and Mark's dad)
One female (Rita)
Three familiar people (Mark, Mark's dad,
    Rita)

DREAM THREE

Two friendly interactions (Richard
    helps D get books and Denise
    helps D get what she needs)
One male (Richard)
One female (Denise)
Two familiar people (Richard,
    Denise)

DREAM FOUR

One aggressive interaction (some men
    try to beat up D)
Three friendly interactions (Phil holds
    baby, D holds baby, Phil will help D)
Two males (Phil, some men—note that a
    group of people counts as one character)
One female (cousin)
Two familiar characters (Phil, cousin)
One stranger (some men)

TOTALS:

1) Aggressor: 1
2) D is aggressor: 0
3) Victim: 0

4) D is victim: 0
5) Someone is friendly: 7
6) Males: 6

7) Females: 4
8) Familiar: 8
9) Strangers: 2

As you can see, Chris is, indeed, a female!

As discussed in the previous section, these four categories contain the building blocks of everyone's dreams: misfortune, groups, aggression, and few emotions (more on emotions in the next chapter). But on this basic structure of dreaming unfolds the insights into your own unique and creative self to which your dreams will lead you.

In Chris's dreams there are several people who are trying to help: these are dream characters who can benefit her in her work. An ally in the dream world is someone to become acquainted with. We explore helpful dream characters in part III of this book.

You may want to use the following checklist and table with your own dreams. The more dreams you include, the better.

DREAM NUMBER

1	2	3	4	5	6	7	8	9	10	TOTAL	
—	—	—	—	—	—	—	—	—	—	———	1) Someone (not D) is aggressive
—	—	—	—	—	—	—	—	—	—	———	2) D is aggressive
—	—	—	—	—	—	—	—	—	—	———	3) Someone (not D) is a victim of aggression
—	—	—	—	—	—	—	—	—	—	———	4) D is a victim of aggression
—	—	—	—	—	—	—	—	—	—	———	5) Someone is friendly
—	—	—	—	—	—	—	—	—	—	———	6) Number of males
—	—	—	—	—	—	—	—	—	—	———	7) Number of females
—	—	—	—	—	—	—	—	—	—	———	8) Number of people D knows
—	—	—	—	—	—	—	—	—	—	———	9) Number of strangers

Are your dreams like those of the typical man or woman? Or are they more androgynous? If the latter is true, you are probably integrating masculine and feminine dreaming patterns into your dream life, in true creative style. More characteristics of famous creative people that may be reflected in your dreams are revealed in chapter 3.

What Do Dreams Tell Us about People?

We tend to dream about the matters that concern us when we are awake: our work, our friends, our families, our homes, and our loves. Studies on dreams and personality show that, although the architecture of dreams is pretty much the same for everyone, certain dream elements are more prevalent among certain kinds of people.

For example, research I performed at the University of California at Berkeley found that sociable people have more people in their dreams and interact with them more often than do people who would rather keep to themselves, and physically aggressive people have more violent dreams than do most people.[8]

Keep in mind that these studies are concerned with the general population and the "average" person within a group (the average aggressive person, the average sociable person). But who wants to find oneself trapped inside a statistic? Findings and theories can be interesting and useful, but they can also diminish the personal meaningfulness of our own dreams. All of the findings about dreaming presented here so far should be used as a guide against which to compare your own dreams, helping you to identify those which are most unusual. Those artful dreams will provide you with the richest possibilities for insight.

British writer John Ruskin transcribed in his diary "the ghastliest nightmare of a dream I ever had in my life." This dream (below) serves as a metaphorically apt warning to us of the dangers of too much intellectual interpretation. As we will see in the next chapter, it is best to stay with feelings rather than rely too heavily on "heady" theories.

> ...I went to *rest* myself into a room full of fine old pictures; the first of which, when I examined it—and it was

large—was of an old surgeon dying by dissecting himself!
It was worse than dissecting—*tearing*: and with circum-
stances of horror about the treatment of the head which
I will not enter.[9]

D. H. Lawrence, in a letter to Katherine Mansfield, writes of
the integrity of dreams:

> I dreamed such a vivid little dream of you last night…It
> was night, and very starry. We looked at the stars, and
> they were different. All the constellations were different,
> and I, who was looking for Orion, to show you, because
> he is rising now, was very puzzled by these thick, close,
> brilliant new constellations. Then suddenly we saw one
> planet, so beautiful, a large, fearful, strong star, that we
> were both pierced by it, possessed, for a second. Then I
> said, 'That's Jupiter'—but I felt that it wasn't Jupiter—at
> least not the everyday Jupiter.
>
> Ask Jung or Freud about it? Never! It was a star that
> blazed for a second on one's soul.[10]

Humbly Observing Your Dream World

The boundaries between dreaming and waking can become confused, especially for those who create, who dream vividly and use
dreams in their creative work. The creative process can also take
on dreamlike qualities, with normal perceptions of time and space
distorted. When lecturing on dreams, I address the strange floating
line between wakefulness and dreaming by asking students how
they know they are awake and not dreaming.

Hands go up and students boldly offer their replies:

"Because when I'm dreaming, things aren't like they are when I'm awake. And right now, they are. So I'm awake."

"How do you know? Maybe you're dreaming now, and only think things are as you think they are when you're awake," I say.

"When I'm awake, my feelings are more vivid and real."

"Is that from inside the dream, or from outside the dream? And how do you know whether you're inside or outside now? As Bertrand Russell said, 'I do not now believe that I am dreaming but I cannot prove that I am not.'"

Stephen LaBerge, an expert on lucid dreaming, once explained to me that, in fact, all you have to do to know whether you are dreaming or awake is to focus on something, turn your gaze away, then refocus on the same object. If you are dreaming, the object will change.

I tried this trick in what I thought was a dream. I looked at a table, looked away, and then back again. The table stayed steady when I refocused upon it. Since then, I've never been absolutely sure I wasn't dreaming. Still, I write down what seem to be my dreams anyway, just in case.

□ ～～ □ ～～ □

Now, enter the dreamscape that will guide you through the book. Relax and lead yourself into the meadow. . .

The morning is crisp and clear. Far off, you can just make out the line of trees that seems to be beckoning, waiting. A wide, open space stretches in the sun between you and the woods. You know you must cross it before nightfall, but it is a long way, and you do not know what you will find there . . . Perhaps if you just sit for a little while and enjoy the view. Perhaps just a little nap. . .

≈ Chapter 2 ≈

Emotion in Dreams: A Key to Meaning

I think dreams are important in terms of how they assist you creatively.
They can help clarify an emotional condition…You might
have a dream where your true emotional state is revealed.

—*Maurice Sendak*[11]

EMOTIONS YOU EXPERIENCE (or don't) in your dream might be the most important clue to its meaning. Start to pay attention to the emotions you and the other characters feel in your dreams, and note when you would expect to feel a feeling if the same situation were happening in waking life.

In the last chapter, we discovered that the things we do in our dreams are much like the things we do, or think about doing, while awake. Thomas Nashe wrote more than 400 years ago in "The Terrors of the Night":

> . . . as an arrow which is shot out of a bow is sent forth many times with such force that it flieth far beyond the mark whereat it was aimed, so our thoughts, intensively fixed all the daytime upon a mark we are to hit, are now and then overdrawn with such force that they fly beyond the mark of the day into the confines of the night.[12]

While often filled with strange and bizarre imagery, dreams do mirror waking life concerns, thoughts, and behavior. Looking at your dream journal can be like looking into a clear pond at your own face, into your own eyes, seeing there just what you do and think while awake.

When you are creating, this reflection can be especially illuminating. To read over your dreams the next morning—or months or even years later—means that you are witnessing your life. You learn which actions and attitudes seemed to help or hinder you, what obstacles you faced, and how you overcame or avoided them. But dreams are more like allegorical films than documentaries. Even when they seem most literally to echo real life, they hint at more, speaking in their own deep language. To understand them on this level, you need to know how they differ most from waking experience.

One key to dreams' helpfulness rests at the wood's murky edge, which dapples, now dark, now light. You look and wonder what resides there. You feel curious, or perhaps fearful or on guard as you begin to cross the meadow toward the wood. . .

What is most different between dreams and life? The answer surprises at first: although we do and think the same things while dreaming as we do and think while awake, we do not feel in dreams the way we say we feel while awake.

Psychologists who have worked with the dreams of many clients discovered that one way to find out what a dream means for its creator is to offer an interpretation and then see whether it gets a strong "aha!" response—an immediate sense of *Yes! That is what it means!* The correct interpretation brings feeling to the surface.

Feelings within the dream are the most important part of dreaming.[13] Listening to your dreams can help you attend to your emotions. In dreams, you can find yourself in strange surroundings that seem oddly normal or in familiar territory made somehow strange. You may suffer catastrophes without blinking. A terrifying, drooling monster comes after you and you calmly run. Or you are frightened, but in your fear, you cannot move.

Clinical experience and research show that we typically tend to experience different emotions in our dreaming and waking lives.[14] For instance:

- People who say they are sad while awake tend to have happy dreams more often than does the "average" person.

- Those who say they are happy while awake have sad dreams more often than average.

- People who tend to rely on facts, figures, and other objective criteria to make decisions have dreams full of feeling.

• Those who most often make their decisions based upon their hearts have fewer feelings than average in their dreams.

• Frightened individuals living in the midst of a terrifying natural disaster have more happy, carefree dreams than average.

Dreams express the unacknowledged or unfelt side of our emotional lives; this function may be the key to their psychological purpose, and it is definitely an aid to self-insight.

Many famous creative people have recognized the importance of this role of dreams. Maurice Sendak wrote about it in the quote at the beginning of this chapter. W. H. Auden advised, "Learn from your dreams what you lack." Thomas Nashe wrote:

> He that dreams merrily is like a boy new breeched, who leaps and danceth for joy his pain is passed. But long that joy stays not with him for presently after, his master, the day, seeing him so jocund and pleasant, comes and does as much for him again, whereby his hell is renewed.[15]

Writer Amy Tan described a dream in which she was being chased by something. She was frightened—a clue to pay close attention to the circumstances surrounding her fear, and her response to it. The more she tried to run away, the harder it became to flee. Then a friend appeared who had recently died. He told her to turn and see what was coming after her. Although she feared the thing would kill her, she courageously risked her life by turning around, and her pursuer disappeared.[16]

This is a powerful emotional dream with an important message. We have all had frightening dreams of being chased by someone who seems to be trying to harm us. The last thing we want to do is to stop and meet the pursuer. However, as Amy Tan learned, if we turn and face what is coming after us, it loses its power. In chapter 8, we will explore how something pursuing us often reflects a neglected part of ourselves that is trying to make contact. For now, remember that dream emotions are the first and most important key to use in unlocking our dreams.

Emotions and Water in Dreams

After author John Nichols got divorced, he dreamed about watering fields outside of the house in which he lived with his ex-wife. Although he tried to stop it, the water in his dream became out of control and flooded the area.[17]

Just as emotions are a key to a dream's meaning, so too is water a universal element and the only cross-cultural dream image dream experts agree about. Water represents the source of life and, psychologically, our deepest, unconscious emotions. John Nichols's recurring dream was about his feelings—his fear of losing control of his own overwhelming emotions.

Jessica, a filmmaker, dreamed the following dream midway through her therapy, when she was trying to overcome a self-defeating pattern that prevented her from maintaining success in her field:

> I am in the neighborhood where I grew up. I'm going to see Leah (my childhood best friend, who is now really successful at what she does). I realize I have a long way to walk, and it will take me a long time. I'm trying to reach the beach. It's been such a long walk already. I get to the bluff and the tide is in. The houses are all abandoned and partially demolished. There are few left. The tide comes in and washes over the road and the road becomes a beach. I slosh through the waves and then realize I need to be on shore and keep walking.

What would the water in Jessica's dream indicate about her emotions? She speaks of tides, water that ebbs and flows. It blocks her path, but she moves through it.

Jessica's dream was one in a series in which she came in contact with the ocean, which was sometimes dangerous, sometimes calm and inviting. As she has been able to feel her emotions more completely, building inner strength in order to do so, Jessica has come to fear her feelings less. She knows that by being willing to acknowledge her emotions a bit at a time, she protects herself from becoming overwhelmed by them. Her dream shows that, rather than getting in too deeply, she realizes she needs to move into her feelings more slowly, to stay "grounded" and in touch with what is familiar and solid, as she explores the edges of her emotional life.

Jessica's dream contrasts with that of John Nichols, who tries to build something to contain the emotions. Jessica may actually need to build more protection for herself from her overwhelming feelings, whereas John Nichols's walls may be too strong—he may need to allow himself to feel more. Of course, we should never make inferences based on only one dream. These dreams only serve as examples of patterns you may see in your own dream life. The more dreams you have recorded in your dream journal, the better—ten is a good start.

A month later, after continuing to explore her feelings safely within the therapeutic setting, Jessica had this dream:

> I am in the ocean near shore with someone else—a young man. Godzilla shows up, emerging from the water. I place myself in danger for a minute in order to get a closer look, knowing I can get out before getting eaten. I study Godzilla, then dash out and walk away, down the beach.

Jessica starts off in the water, and who should appear from the depths but Godzilla! Of which emotion might Jessica be beginning to be aware, and in this case, to use in her life?

The dream seemed to continue several months later:

> I'm in a house with a young woman. I admire her. She has all of these really stylish movie-promo posters on the walls. A Godzilla-like creature is there, too, except that he's friendly; he's changed. First, he transforms into a blob, then a child's toy, then this harmless creature. I'm trying to draw Godzilla for him so he can transform into Godzilla again and scare off someone bothering us. He doesn't know what he looked like before. I tried to compare him to a Tyrannosaurus Rex, but he didn't know what that was, either. He seems willing to help, but he's just not sure how to look like or act like Godzilla.

At this point, Jessica had begun to feel her anger ("my least favorite emotion") in her waking life. She couldn't remember the last time she had felt angry. "It was probably when I was three or four and had a toy taken away." As is the case with many adults who survived abusive childhoods, Jessica identified her anger with her abuser's, and vowed never to become like him. She believed that anger and violence were the same thing. She had lost the capacity to express her justifiable anger; she didn't know how to be Godzilla. Many of her dreams had anger in them, but it was expressed by other characters, and usually directed at her. This next dream, another month later, showed a change:

> I am in this older, gray-haired woman's house. She has fixed gourmet lunches for everyone else but me. I think how unfair this is and get angry. I do have a glass of clear, cool water, which is nice, but it isn't lunch. This woman has rejected me. She doesn't like me. But she doesn't even know me! So I go up to her and explain that my feelings are hurt. At first, she's very cold, puttering around in her kitchen. She serves me some easy, bad-tasting food. She opens a cabinet and I see collections of futuristic-looking videotapes. She asks if I've ever seen them. I say no, but am clearly fascinated. "Oh!" she says, happily. I see she must be lonely here. I begin to look through the tapes and say, "You see? We are on the same side!" We talk and I'm pleased. So is she. Something is reconciled. She just didn't know what I'm like.

In this dream, Jessica's emotions (the glass of water) are contained and clear. As we see in a later chapter, dream characters can represent parts of ourselves, and the "old woman" has been with Jessica a long time, a critical and cold force, rejecting her. Now, Jessica gets angry, and when she directly tells the woman how she feels, the situation changes. The old woman transforms from critical and withholding to being the guardian of Jessica's creativity, keeping the videotapes, waiting for Jessica to come to them. Jessica now has a helpful dream figure to aid her in the expression of her creativity (more about such figures in part III). As it happened, the old woman returned to Jessica's dream world whenever Jessica began to neglect her creative life, reminding her to continue toward her future.

Dream Metaphors for Specific Feelings

Sometimes we have dreams in which it seems we should feel an emotion, but do not. Our dreams are full of pictorial metaphors that express our feelings, particularly when they are not directly felt within the dream. Using metaphors to express emotion is not something we do only in our dreams. As psycholinguist Dr. Raymond Gibbs wrote in his book, *Poets of the Mind,* each of us will use more than 260 million metaphors over a sixty-year life span in ordinary conversation, most of them when talking about our emotional experience.[18] Because language relies so heavily upon the use of metaphor, especially when we are expressing how we feel, it makes sense that we use metaphors to describe emotion in dreams as well.

We have few feelings in our dreams as compared to our waking life, and the dream emotion we most often feel is apprehension or upset. Looking at your own dreams, you may find that one emotion creeps into your dreams more often than others. "Favored" dream emotions, including anger, fear, joy, sadness, and guilt, can tell you quite a lot about yourself.

Apprehension (fear, worry)

We saw how John Nichols' and Jessica's fears were represented by water symbolism in their dreams. Fear and worry are often symbolized by water: rising tides, tsunamis or other waves, flooding.

Anger

When we are angry, we say things like, "I'm so mad I could burst!" or "He just exploded at me!" or "It's burning me up!" Another psycholinguist, George Lakoff, notes that anger is often metaphorically described in speech as a heated fluid in a container that is in danger of bursting.[19]

Imagine you are dreaming the following dream:

> It is night. You are standing near a fire with several other people. You are cooking something over the fire, a stew of some kind. As you watch, the stew bubbles over and suddenly the pot in which it was cooking shatters. You are not hurt, but there is no more stew. You awaken, realizing you felt nothing at all in the dream.

If you were actually standing there near something bubbling over, you might do something other than just watch. In any case, you would probably feel something when the pot broke. How strange that, in the dream, you did not. Because you did not feel something in the dream that would invoke a feeling in real life, this would be a dream to explore further.

If we look at the dream images as metaphors, it appears this dreamer is "stewing" over something that is going to bubble over and burst unless the dreamer pays attention to it. Remember that the way we feel while dreaming is different from the way we say we feel when awake. Because there's no feeling within this dream, perhaps what's going to burst is the dreamer's feeling, out of the container where it has been hiding.

According to Lakoff's observations, it may well be that this dreamer is angry and is afraid to acknowledge and express the full force of her anger. Her feelings are stewing, about to bubble over. They are so strong, she could just burst! The dream is a picture of what she is feeling. It also shows her that it is possible for her to express her feelings without harming herself.

In reality, the person who had this dream is an artist, plagued by a series of similar dreams of explosions, fires, and breaking glass. She had this dream at a time when she was questioning her association with a group of people who, she said, "couldn't care less about what I do artistically." After we talked about the dream, she began to feel tightness in her stomach (where anger often hides), and then realized how angry she was at her friends (and her family, as it turned out) for being unwilling or unable to support her artistic work. Her anger led to action: she spoke with her friends about her frustration, began to consciously seek out a new creative community (more on the importance of such communities in chapter 11), and became more aware of her tendency to devalue her own talent, in much the same way the group of people in her dream had done.

Lisa's dream also has an image of heated fluid in a container, which is combined with the water element discussed in the previous section.

> I was with a group of scientists on an Arctic expedition. We had set up a lab/sleeping place in the middle of this rock that came up out of the ocean. It was very light inside the rock, and there was a pool in the center through which we could dive to get outside. We had just woken up and someone suggested that we go to the hot spring nearby. I asked if anyone else wanted to go nude, since I was feeling so comfortable about being there and being myself. Carl said he would, but one of the girls seemed kind of shocked at me. I felt somewhat ashamed. Then we were at the hot spring, which was a warm pool in the center of another rock nearby, but this one was open to the sky. The water was blue-green and very clear. I felt very good being in it, but then realized I had a real hard time staying afloat in it. I kept choking on the water. Then we were swimming back to our rock. The sky was very dark, but there was a shimmering light over the darkness of the ocean. Swimming was much easier than it had been in the hot spring. Once I thought our rock was moving away or we were being swept away from it, but it was just an illusion.

What might the water in this dream represent? The hot spring image comes after she describes the other woman in the dream as shocked. Perhaps Lisa, an actor and a writer, is struggling to overcome feelings of shame, as demonstrated by the other woman's judgment. (In a later chapter, we learn how others' emotions can mirror our own.) In her dreams, Lisa is willing to express herself as she is. Shedding her persona (clothes) in spite of another's distaste, she dives into the emotions residing in her center. She courageously enters the hot-fluid-in-a-container (anger) and safely swims away again through the dark ocean. In the dream, Lisa recognizes that her fear of being overpowered by her feelings is only an illusion.

Sadness and Joy

Sadness is also frequently expressed metaphorically in language, and the equivalent images are sometimes represented in our dreams. Sadness is "down": "I'm really down in the dumps"; "I'm in low spirits"; "You're down and out." When we dream of being in deep valleys, or when our dream selves journey downward, it can represent sadness. Happiness, though, is "up": "I feel higher than a kite"; "What an uplifting experience!"; "Cheer up"; "Her mood is rising." Our flying dreams are typically happy dreams.

Dr. Gibbs surmises that these associations of sadness with down and happiness with up come from our early experiences with those who cared for us. We looked up to them because they were physically above us, they lifted us up and cared for us. When we mature, down is below us, and we associate it with being inferior and childlike.[20] Colors can also be associated with mood. In the West, we describe dour sad moods as the color blue. Picasso painted his series of blue-toned works during his depressive periods.[21] I have noticed that depressed individuals often represent their mood in dreams by dreaming of being in a blue room, or of wearing blue clothing: "I'm cloaked in blue." Black is the color of mourning in the West, whereas in the East, white is associated with death.

Guilt

What is the image that comes to mind when you think of guilt? For most people, it is a burden of some kind. "I feel weighed down"; "When I apologized, I felt a great weight lifted off of my shoulders."

One client of mine who had struggled with the guilt of having, years before, left his family to pursue a solitary artistic life, dreamed that he was climbing from a deep valley up a dry and rocky incline. He repeatedly slipped back down. He realized that he would never make it up the hill with the huge black backpack he was carrying. Unstrapping it, he left it on a ledge and climbed on. When he looked back, the backpack had disappeared. Upon waking, he realized just how guilty and depressed he had been for the last several years. The dream marked the turning point in a long process of apology, self-forgiveness, and acceptance of his chosen path. His mood improved and his creative productivity increased when he was no longer burdened with the guilt that had constrained his ability to do what he loved.

The following exercises may help you identify those emotions you might need to explore.

Exercise: Dream Metaphors for Emotion

Dream images of heated fluid, up, down, weight, and color are not limited to these emotional meanings. Even so, it is worthwhile to ask yourself whether your own dreams contain these elements, and if so, what they might mean about your emotional life.

Look back over your dream journal for instances where you dreamed of a hot fluid in a container of some kind; were burdened; were high or low, or moved from one to the other; or where blue, black, or white appeared. Is there a pattern of such images in your dreams? Do the emotional metaphors associated with these images express something about your own feelings that you might not have previously realized? If so, try to express those feelings in your creative work.

You might want to write down a few notes about them here. Then, come back every few months and compare your dream patterns with what you find—become emotionally refreshed and witness the progress of your own journey.

How Much Feeling Is Too Much or Too Little?

If you are having trouble identifying metaphors for the feelings in your dreams, you might just be dreaming of them directly. We tend to dream about certain emotions more than others, and because those we often express in dreams we tend not to be aware of in waking life, charting our dream emotions can enliven our understanding of our emotional state.

Exercise: Your Emotional Dreams

Here is your opportunity to learn what kind of emotions your dreams tend to include or exclude. Calvin S. Hall and Robert Van de Castle, who developed a system for researching dreams, suggest a number of key words to look for in your written dream reports.[22]

EMOTIONS	DREAM FEELINGS
Anger	annoyed, irritated, mad, provoked, furious, enraged, belligerent, incensed, indignant, jealous, frustrated
Apprehension*	terrified, horrified, frightened, scared, worried, nervous, concerned, panicky, alarmed, uneasy, upset, remorseful, sorry, disgusted, ashamed
Sadness	disappointed, depressed, sad, distressed, hurt, lonely, lost, miserable, hopeless, crushed, heartbroken
Happiness	content, pleased, relieved, amused, cheerful, glad, relaxed, gratified, wonderful, elated, joyful, exhilarated, excited

  * feelings expressing concern about the possibility of physical injury or punishment, social ridicule, or rejection

You will need at least ten recent dreams for this exercise, preferably the last ten dreams you remember, or any unedited set of ten dreams that occurred in a row. Otherwise, you might consciously or unconsciously select dreams of a certain kind and this exercise would then not be able to give you a true picture of your emotional dream life.

Read over your dreams. First, jot down on a sheet of paper the feelings (anger, apprehension, sadness, happiness) that you felt within the dream. In this stage, you are looking for certain words we typically use to describe our feelings. Write down every feeling that occurred in each dream. Then, check the table on page 32 to see with which emotion each emotion word corresponds. Tally up and then total the number of times you experienced each emotion across all of the dreams. Which one did you experience the most? For most people, it is apprehension.

EMOTION WORDS	TALLY ACROSS DREAMS	TOTAL
Anger		
Apprehension		
Sadness		
Happiness		

Divide the total number of "apprehensions" (in the "total" column) by the total number of all emotions you experienced. Compare that number (a percentage) to the norm, or average amount of apprehension people feel in dreams as shown in the table on page 34. For example, if you had two sad feelings, one happy one, zero angry ones, and six apprehensive ones in ten dreams, your apprehension percentage would be $6/9 = .67$, or 67 percent. You would have more apprehension in your dreams than does the average person.

What about your second most frequent emotion, or your least frequent emotion? Do the same calculations for them as you did for apprehension, than compare your results with the norms in the table.[23]

AVERAGE FREQUENCY OF DREAM EMOTIONS

	WOMEN	MEN
Anger	15%	20%
Apprehension	45%	43%
Sadness	17%	12%
Happiness	24%	25%

Do you have 15 percent more or less of any of these emotions than the percentages in the table? If so, those are the feelings you may want to explore more in depth. If the amount for a particular emotion is less than in the table, you might want to ask yourself whether you characteristically feel that emotion in waking life. Do you feel it more strongly and more pervasively than the others? Are there situations in your dreams in which that emotion would seem appropriate, if the event were happening in your waking life? If an emotion occurs more frequently in your dreams than it does in the table, you might consider whether that is an emotion you might want to become more aware of in your waking life. Again, note the situations in your dreams in which this emotion occurs. Save your notes for the sections on the dream themes of famous creative people in chapter 3.

As you have seen, the emotions you favor in your dreams show much about you that you might not otherwise be aware of. It would be wise to listen, for the emotions you feel (or don't feel) in your dreams may lead you to recognize something vital about your deep self.

In the next chapter, you will discover how your dreams reflect creativity.

You awaken. The scents of spring grasses and wet earth bring a smile. Chirping birds flash overhead, their feathers caught in the shafts of light not yet obscured by the distant wood. You stretch and rise, noticing people milling about what could be circus tents. You walk toward them and stop at a long table of aromatic food. A group a bit apart from the rest is busily crafting poems, stories, plans, music, and art. Someone else sits alone, shrouded in an atmosphere of sadness or loss. Children weave between the others. You head toward them all, hoping to be welcomed. . .

≋ Chapter 3 ≋

Creative Dreams and Dreamers

As morning is born
the peony blushes,
the clouds billow,
the earth moves,
the birds soar,
the leaves on the trees
dance in the wind.

and I am alone
and motionless
with my dreams.

—*Laurel Burch*

Who Is the Creative Dreamer?

Here is one dream from a woman who spends a lot of her waking life doing creative activities, and another from a person who has little interest in creating (she most enjoys other pursuits):

Susan's dream:

> Someone or some sort of group was chasing me and I kept looking for the entrance to a cave that was in some unfamiliar elementary school. I knew if I found the cave, I could elude my pursuers and remain safe. I never found the cave's entrance. I was scared.

Anne's dream:

> I was at my friend's house where I was staying for the night. I dreamed that I had to get up out of bed and went to the couch in the living room to read.

Can you guess which dreamer is which?

Although it portrays a common theme, that of being chased by a group (see chapter 1), Susan's dream introduces an original element: a cave in an elementary school. She is the dreamer who loves to create. As we shall see in this chapter, originality and anxiety, among other things, mark the dreams of people who like to be creative and nourish that quality in their waking lives.

Before reading further, take out your dream journal and read through your most recent dreams. Then relax, close your eyes, and recall them in as much detail as you can. For some people, it is easier to recapture the dream by imagining you are descending a staircase, with each step down bringing you closer to it.

The following exercise measures the number of elements in your dreams that are common to people who enjoy using their creativity. The more dreams you have, the more accurately this exercise will reflect your dream life. Try to remember at least ten dreams (twenty is better!).

Checklist: Your Creative Dreams

For each dream, place a mark beside each element (a–g) that occurs in that dream. Resist the strong temptation to impose what you are now thinking and feeling about the dream upon what actually happened in the dream.

YOUR DREAM ELEMENTS

TALLY   TOTAL

___ a)   ___ children (age twelve and younger)
___ b)   ___ natural body of water (lakes, rivers, waterfalls, and so forth)
___ c)   ___ sexuality (sexual thoughts or physical expression)
___ d)   ___ apprehension (see page 32)*
___ e)   ___ original plot (as compared with a short story or novel)
___ f)   ___ bizarreness (dream is quite unlike real life)
___ g)   ___ creativity (famous creative people, creative works, doing something creative)

  * When tallying occurrences of apprehension, make sure not to infer emotion based on how you would feel if you were in that situation in waking life. Check only if the feeling was actually experienced in the dream.

Total up the number of marks next to each item. Divide each total by the number of dreams you included. Write this result (a percentage) in the column headed "Your Dreams."[24]

YOUR DREAMS	THEIR DREAMS (WOMEN)	THEIR DREAMS (MEN)
___ a) children	4%	2%
___ b) natural body of water	9%	2%
___ c) sexuality	4%	10%
___ d) apprehension	45%	43%
___ e) originality	10%	10%
___ f) bizarreness	63%	61%
___ g) creativity	3%	2%
___ average # of dreams I remember in a week, when I try	1 per week	1 per week

For example, if three of ten dreams you included had natural bodies of water in them, you would write 30 percent (3 divided by 10) on the line next to item (b).

In the columns headed "Their Dreams" are the number of times the average (that word again!) man or woman dreams of the element in a series of one hundred dreams. For example, the average woman mentions a natural body of water about nine times in every hundred dreams. Compare your results with the percentages in these columns. If your number on any given element is higher, that means you dream about it more often than do most people. If your number is lower, you dream about the element less often.

Place a star beside any element of yours that is at least 15 percent greater or less than the comparable number in the "Their Dreams" column. Statistically speaking, this is a difference that is not likely to have occurred by chance.

What Extraordinarily Creative People's Dreams Are Like

What do these numbers mean? Well, some of the elements mean nothing special. As a person who enjoys creating, your dreams are probably not any more bizarre than anyone else's. You may tend to be more emotionally expressive than others (one study showed that imaginative people are more likely to cry in joy or sorrow than are others), but your dreams do not contain more water. The other elements do occur less (sexuality) or more often (children, apprehension, originality, creativity, better recall) in the dreams of people who create than in others' dreams.

Fear and Trembling

> . . . *night after night—surprised by sleep, while I struggled to remain awake, starting up to bless my own loud screams that had awakened me—yea, dear friends! Till my repeated night-yells had made me a nuisance in my own house.* As I live and am a man, this is an unexaggerated tale—my dreams become the substances of my life.
>
> —*Samuel Taylor Coleridge*, Notebooks[25]

> . . . last night was just such a noisy night of horrors, as three nights out of four are, with me. O God! when a man blesses the loud scream of agony that awakes him, night after night, night after night—and when a man's repeated night-screams have made him a nuisance in his own house, it is better to die than to live.
>
> —*Samuel Taylor Coleridge, Letter to R. Southey, 1803*[26]

As the poet Coleridge knew firsthand, people who create tend to have more apprehensive dreams than do other people. Sometimes (as illustrated in chapter 4), these intense dreams provide the inspiration for a creative work, as they have for Anne Rice, C. S. Lewis, Robert Louis Stevenson, Emily Brontë, and many others.

The creative life fosters apprehension. It is difficult to balance the other responsibilities in our lives with the responsibility to create. We may try to ignore our doubts about our ability to continue, the value of our work, or how others might receive it. For instance, Maya Angelou has frightening dreams when her writing is going badly: "Would I have a good dream when the work is going badly? No. No such thing. It just seems they tell the truth."[27] We need to be aware of our anxious feelings, consider what is causing them, and then move beyond them. Perhaps we have so much apprehension in our dreams because we must continually face our unconscious anxious feelings in order to transform them into a creative product.

The classical dream theories of Sigmund Freud and Carl Jung offer explanations for our preponderance of dream anxiety.[28] Freud believed that creativity and dreams both involve the transformation of anxiety-provoking sexual and aggressive wishes and fears. We channel our anxiety into our creative work without having to completely feel it. Carl Jung described creativity as an unconscious negotiation with the anxiety-generating part of the psyche that contains all of those aspects of ourselves of which we are unaware. He believed that creativity requires the strength to recognize unpleasant aspects of the self, with the goal of acceptance and integration of them into our self-image. Creative work requires plummeting to the depths of the psyche and meeting there all manner of unfamiliar beasts (see chapter 8).

As you will discover in the next chapter, most psychologists agree that anxiety is a necessary ingredient of the creative process. Your dreams force you to come face to face with your fears so that you may continue to do what you love best.

Better Recall

On average, people who create remember one-third more dreams than do others.[29] Recall can ebb and flow, however. Although Maya Angelou remembers more dreams while writing, Stephen King recalls fewer. Jungian analysts find that when their clients are using a storylike imagery technique in therapy (active imagination), they recall fewer dreams. Maya Angelou considers herself an autobiographer. Perhaps the number of dreams we remember varies inversely with the degree to which we use our imaginations while creating.

Creative Pursuits

Those who make new things or produce new ideas tend to dream about their own creative pursuits, prominent creative people, and famous works. Sometimes they will dream about a particular mentor, either living or dead, who will occasionally offer encouragement or indirect advice. The poet Walt Whitman reported a dream in which he saw a ship in a storm at midnight, on the deck of which stood:

> . . . a slender, slight, beautiful figure, a dim man, apparently enjoying all the terror, the murk, and the dislocation of which he was the center and the victim. That figure of

my lurid dream might stand for Edgar Poe, his spirit, his fortunes, and his poems themselves all lurid dreams.[30]

In the dream, Poe is comfortable with fear and chaos, and his appearance here might have had something to do with Whitman's own feelings about chaos and confusion, making them seem more acceptable.

British novelist Graham Greene dreamed of a number of famous writers, among them Henry James, T. S. Eliot, W. H. Auden, and D. H. Lawrence. In one dream, James helped Greene to press on, despite the dreamer's wanting to quit writing. The other authors questioned, challenged, or praised Greene's own work in his dreams.[31]

Vivid Dreams

Those who create also have extraordinarily vivid dreams. The French painter Frederic Mistral illustrated this quality when describing a dream of irises in his memoirs:

> In a lovely stream of water which wound all round the farmhouse, a limpid, transparent, azure stream like the waters of the fountain at Vaucluse, I beheld the most beautiful clumps of iris covered with a perfect wonder of golden blossoms! Little dragonflies with blue silk wings came and settled on the flowers, while I swam about naked in the laughing rivulet and plucked by handfuls and armsful of those enchanting yellow blooms. And the more I picked the more sprang up.[32]

A dream such as this may make us wonder whether our dreams are really so original, or whether their compelling quality is simply due to the storytelling ability of the dreamer, having nothing to do with the dream as it really occurred. Having researched this idea, I found that when we remember or write down our dreams, we are really telling ourselves a story about a story we created during the night. We cannot remember our dreams perfectly or in every detail; however, the dream stories we remember and write down are different from stories we might make up during the day. They contain different elements and themes than do the stories or images we create. [33]

Those who create in their waking lives may tell better stories than other people and their dreams do have more original "plots." As he transcribed it, Mistral's dream is a sort of painting, invoking a rich, visual scene. Written by someone else, though, it might have read:

> I dreamed of a stream and a farmhouse and beautiful yellow irises. Dragonflies landed on them. I swam naked in the water and picked many blossoms. The more I picked, the more appeared.

Though a less impressive tale than Mistral's version, this is still an unusual story, reflecting the unusual mind of its creator.

Sexual Dreams

Because sexuality in dreams is such an important (and fun!) topic, it will be discussed more thoroughly in chapter 10. For now, though, it can be generalized that people who like to create have slightly less sexuality in their dreams than others. When we do have a sexual dream, we are most likely creating during the day.

Children and Loss

Not only do people who create have more original, vivid, and apprehensive dreams, they also tend to have more child characters, and experience more loss in their dream lives. We explore these dreams of children and loss in the next chapter on the development of creativity.

◻ ≋ ◻ ≋ ◻

So far, we have found that people who like to create tend to remember more of their dreams. They have fewer sexual dreams overall (except when creating), dream more original and apprehensive dreams, have more child characters, and experience more loss in dreams than do others. In later chapters, we expand these elements into dream themes that can help you explore and unlock your creativity.

Next, we look at some of the challenges posed by the creative life.

People Who Create

What is essentially mysterious cannot yield itself to scrutiny.
—*Frank Barron*

Those who like to be creative have concerns related to our creativity that tend to appear in dreams. So far, you have seen how the dreams of people who create are similar to anyone else's dreams and how they are different. Because those who attempt to create new and original things and ideas are, by definition, unique, their psychological needs and motivations sometimes run counter to those of society.

In a series of studies that are now classics in the field of psychology, researchers at the University of California at Berkeley's Institute of Personality Assessment and Research (IPAR) studied creative writers, architects, mathematicians, scientists, business managers, and artists who became famous (and people with similar lives and vocations who were not famous or not yet famous). Most of these people either were, or became, extraordinarily successful. The IPAR research revealed that prominent creative people have certain characteristics in common. These qualities are more likely to belong to famous creative people than to others.[34] No one knows whether pursuing the creative life led to the development of these qualities, or whether the qualities facilitated wanting to become successful in the world being willing to do what was necessary to achieve that.

In order for people to be successful in terms of recognition and fame during their lives, society must be ready for their creative work. The contribution of financial resources and social support is of profound importance, as well. No matter how ripe your creativity may be, the world in which you live ultimately plays a tremendous part in your eventual success. Paradoxically, a person who creates may be creating something too original for society to recognize at any given time! Therefore, outward success is a questionable measure of the quality and importance of one's creations.

Childhood

*You never paint what you see or think you see. You paint
with a thousand vibrations the blow that struck you.*

—*Nicholas de Stael*

What were extraordinarily successful people's early lives like?

Value Placed on Achievement

Intellectual or creative pursuits were valued at home.[35] The famous
among us were encouraged to excel in school, they read voraciously,
and they often modeled themselves after the heroes and heroines
they met in books. Many did quite poorly in school. Actor Anthony
Hopkins, for instance, said that at school, "I was a dummy. I thought
perhaps I was on the wrong planet...I would sit perplexed, drinking ink."

Home Environment

Of children who grew up to be prominent in their fields, about
85 percent had unhappy homes,[36] including Nobel Prize winners.[37]
As a result, they struggled with anxiety and witnessed conflict.

There is a bright side to a difficult childhood, however: "Without resistance," said Jean Cocteau, "you can do nothing." The personality characteristics that develop as a result of such parenting lend
themselves well, as Gore Vidal notes, to a creative life:

> Hatred of one parent or the other can make an Ivan the
> Terrible or a Hemingway; the protective love, however, of
> two devoted parents can absolutely destroy an artist.[38]

The anxiety felt by children growing up in difficult families gives them the chance to reexperience those feelings as adults in their dreams. Our dreams can immerse us in our pasts, providing us with the opportunity to mine deeply for the feelings and experiences that enliven our creative world.

Loss

As children, 25 percent of extremely successful creative people experienced the loss of a parent before the age of ten, as had 45 per-cent before the age of twenty[39] (a rate three times as high as in the general American population).[40] As Richard Ochse notes in his informative book on creativity, *Before the Gates of Excellence* (Cambridge University Press), adolescent delinquents and suicidal depressives are the only other two groups with rates of childhood bereavement as high as those of well-known creative people's.[41]

A child who loses a parent is more likely to be creative, go to jail, and/or be suicidal than to grow up to be otherwise. Creative expression can therefore be a lifesaving way of dealing with feelings of loss and pain, as well as a way of expressing aspects of ourselves and connecting with others.

Loneliness

Children destined to become prominent creative adults felt iso-lated, often having no friends or only one friend at a time.[42] They were often shy and introverted, preferring to direct their attention to the inner world of imagination and ideas rather than to the outer world of things and people.

Western culture values extraversion more than introversion. But a certain amount of introversion is necessary for creativity, as is the extraverted ability to give up what is produced and share it with the world. Those of us who are introverted may remember ourselves as being the object of jokes and strange glances, being admonished to "go make friends" or "try to be popular." Introverted children often pay dearly for their dispositions, being labeled aloof, cold, withdrawn, or unfriendly, when they really might just be concentrating on their own creative thoughts!

As adults, famous creative people describe their childhood relationships with pets or animals as being stronger than those they had with people. This may be why people who create have fewer people and more animals in their dreams than do others. Many dream experts believe that animals represent the uncivilized parts of ourselves, with which people who create are more in touch.

Illness, Physical Problems

Prominent creative people were slightly more likely than others to have suffered from disease or physical deformity, or to have believed themselves to be physically unattractive as children.[43] The psychologist Alfred Adler believed that early physical struggles in young children create both a sense of inferiority and a need for superiority.[44] These unpleasant feelings produce adults who strive to be seen by others (and, of course, by themselves) as worthwhile. Although no research has focused on the link between dreams, creativity, and self-esteem, I have noticed that issues of self-worth are particularly common in the dreams of people who create.

Those who like to create and did not have happy childhoods are in good company! If you were fortunate enough to have had a happy childhood, so much the better. Those who did not might be comforted to know that you do not need to have had your basic needs fulfilled as a child, or to have had doting parents who offered you unconditional positive regard, in order to become an expressive, creative adults.

Most everyone dreams about their childhood from time to time. This can take the form of either a setting from childhood ("my childhood house"), a person from way back when, or even of oneself as a child. People who create dream more often of places from childhood than do other people (called *age regression* in dreams), allowing them to step back in time and witness what they experienced so long ago, with many of their feelings and thoughts of that time. In those dreams, we visit the kind of children we were and also the kind of children we have become, for the child within us never ages.

The child is a potent creative symbol in dreams, representing a new part of the psyche, regeneration, and rebirth. Psychologists notice their clients often dream of children when going through major transitions. Most of my clients who enjoy their creativity dream of children when they are about to embark upon a new project.

Famous creative people also discuss their work using the metaphor of pregnancy and birth. As Maurice Sendak describes it,

> It's like you have all these quickie pregnancies—lots of miscarriages. You may want this project to go to full term for all kinds of reasons, but if it doesn't satisfy something inwardly then you ain't gonna have the baby. No matter how you prepare the nursery.[45]

Creative dreamers' tendency to have more children in their dreams, and other themes involving these childhood experiences and how they interact with one another, are discussed in part II of this book.

Creative Dreamers in Adulthood

*Your work is to discover your work and then
with all your heart to give yourself to it.*
—*Buddhist scripture*

Most well-known creative people felt lost, alone, and isolated as children. But they also learned how to pursue their own interests independently because achievement was important to their families. How did these early experiences influence them as adults?

Intelligence

Are famous creative people smarter than other people? Early studies of "creative geniuses" showed that high intelligence is not enough to produce a successful, creative person.[46]

For example, Charles Darwin was terrible with numbers. Jules-Henri Poincaré, the great French mathematician, took a standardized IQ test and scored as an imbecile. Perhaps he was smarter than the author of the test or the person who conducted it, mystifying them both! Mozart was so consumed by music that rhythms sometimes clouded his speech and writing, as this fragment of a letter to his cousin shows:

> I have received reprieved your letter telling selling me that my uncle carbuncle, my aunt, can't and you too are very well hell. Thank God, we too are in excellent health. Today the letter setter from my papa Ha! Ha! dropped safely into my claws paws. I hope that you too have got shot the note dote which I wrote to you from Manheim. If so, so much the better, better than much so.[47]

Although ungrammatical and hard to follow, when read aloud, Mozart's prose sounds like his music!

Creativity studies do demonstrate that a certain basic level of intelligence is necessary to be able to practice a craft, but above that level, high intelligence as measured by IQ is uncorrelated with creativity, not only in artistic endeavors, but also in science, the military, and business. In short, whether or not we create has little to do with how smart we are. Like Mozart, Poincaré, and Darwin, we do some things better than others, and some quite exceptionally well.

Prominent creative adults do tend to be mentally flexible and open to new ideas and unusual experiences (including dreaming). They have a strong aesthetic sense, valuing the form of their creations, the elegance of their theories, and the beauty of their equations. Their dreams are full of color, and painters, in particular, describe their dream landscapes in aesthetic terms.

Independence

Just as when they were children, prominent creative people are self-reliant, would rather work independently, and prefer their own company much of the time, especially when creating.[48] Other people describe them as "reserved" and "aloof." They do not wait for others to tell them what to do or how to do it, for they dislike conformity and want to go their own way. Those whose families exerted strict control and were authoritarian may become rebellious as they grow up. Those whose parents neglected them may develop a deep need to be recognized at almost any cost. We have all heard stories or seen famously exhibitionistic, wildly creative people. Their early lives may explain why they want to be seen, recognized, and valued, and why they abhor being ignored, misunderstood, or controlled. Of course, some are quietly industrious and serious, melting into the background of a group, much as they might have done as children.

Not surprisingly, successful creative adults may have a hard time forming and maintaining warm connections with others. There is nothing wrong or unhealthy about being alone, and this ability is actually related to emotional maturity.

Emotional Instability

In psychology, "normal" most often means average. So what is unusual is, by definition, not normal. Prominent artists and writers tend to be psychologically unusual.[49] For example, in a study of Icelandic great creators, one-third were found to be emotionally unstable. Another study on this topic involved 19,000 people (including famous artists, scientists, and their families) over twenty-six years. Of those who become seriously mentally ill, artists tended to display signs of disordered thinking, whereas scientists tended to suffer extreme mood swings. All of the well-known creative people, be they artists or scientists, had more relatives who had been diagnosed with the serious mental illness of manic-depressive disorder than did the general population.[50]

Paradoxically, though, creative people have more inner resources that help them cope with their inner difficulties. As Frank Barron frequently noted, people who create are both more and less sane ("normal!") than everyone else. Their backgrounds require them to develop strength of character and the ability to delay pressure, to concentrate and persevere, and to rely on themselves. Creative work provides a way to find meaning in one's experience and seems to provide some protection from emotional difficulties.

As novelist Stephen King's recurring dream shows, dreams and creativity allow us to express and exorcise inner demons:

> I'm working very hard in a little hot room—it seems to be the room where I lived as a teenager—and I'm aware that there's a madwoman in the attic. There's a little tiny door under the eave that goes to the attic and I have to finish my work. I have to get that work done or she'll come out and get me. At some point in the dream that door always bursts open and this hideous woman—with all this white hair stuck up around her head like a gone-to-seed dandelion—jumps out with a scalpel. And I wake up.[51]

King's "madwoman in the attic" dream is a perfect illustration of the metaphorical nature of dreaming (the attic symbolizes the head, or unconscious psyche). The author is besieged by this inner figure whenever he is backed up on his work. She seems to be saying, "Create or go mad!" The old woman has no ordinary knife, but a scalpel, which suggests she might be a surgeon, a precise slasher who cuts to heal. Stephen King's madwoman in the attic of his mind, who seems so negative and scary, actually ends up helping him by forcing him to create.

Androgyny

As discussed in chapter 2, people who create are likely to have less stereotypically masculine or feminine interests and personality styles than do others. Because this is so important for dreams, it receives more attention in chapter 10.

Reflect again on your own feelings about masculinity and femininity. Where do you fall on the continuum? Are you more traditionally masculine or feminine? Where on the continuum have your romantic partners been?

Self-Image

Well-known creative people tend to describe themselves as "inventive," "determined," and "enthusiastic," whereas others might describe themselves as "responsible," "reliable," and "sympathetic."[52] People who create present to the world a self-confident face, especially when they become successful. They know they are creative and appreciate their own talents.

Motivation

We have arrived at the essential quality for creativity to flourish. More important than childhood experience, wealth, independence, or anything else, researchers agree that those who create must be dedicated to their work in order to be successful. To put in the amount of time and energy required to learn the skills necessary to be able to express ourselves creatively, we must be motivated from within. We cannot rely upon the support of others to stick to the schedule we make for ourselves, or to isolate ourselves, or to ponder, or to produce, or to dream. We must create our own discipline. As Katharine Hepburn said, "Without discipline, there's no life at all."

People who create are typically less easily satisfied than are other people. They are often ambitious for their work to be recognized by others. They have dreams about work, people who have succeeded in similar fields, and great examples of what they hope to do. You must therefore develop a lifestyle that allows you to create, for the more you produce, the more likely we are to become successful.

Perseverance in the face of numerous rejections or seeming failures characterizes all famous creative people. If they had quit, we would not know of them. In times of trial, they were able to draw upon that inner strength that saw them through to adulthood in order to nourish themselves and replenish the well.

Exercise: Your Creative Self

You might find it valuable to write in your journal about the thoughts and feelings you have had while reading this section. Many of my students and clients are surprised and relieved to find that their history and adult proclivities are so much like those of famous creative people. Their sense of isolation and differentness is eased, and they often find themselves feeling more positive about their creative qualities.

Where We Have Been, Where We Are Going

In part I, you made your way midway across the meadow, considered the journey to come, and learned what you would need to know in order to cross the rest of the way and enter the dark forest. You discovered what kinds of dreams are common to everyone, what famous creative people are like, and what about your own dreams is typical of those who create and what is not. You also learned about the importance of water and feelings in dreams and how to decide to which emotions you may need to pay more attention in your waking life.

Your dreams provide a way to portray your own feelings about your creative work and your relationship with it. In part II, you will explore your own creative process and discover the creative plots in your dreams. You will follow themes that ran through your childhood to meet you in your adult life and in your creative dreams. Then, in part III, you will use all that has come before to journey into the deepest part of the wood, where you will glimpse your own creative process as revealed in your dreams.

☐ ≈ ☐ ≈ ☐

Looking about, you find yourself in the very center of the group. You smile back at each member in turn, wondering what has brought each here to the middle of the meadow. You plan to spend some time with each of them, beginning with the solitary figure at the group's edge, staring quietly toward the forest…Once you have met each of the people in the group, talking a bit and getting to know them, you feel these are your people—they share your history, your way of life, your values. Feeling welcome and at ease, you look about. The one sitting quietly at the edge motions you just past the group to a little dell. The sky is a crystal blue, and the rains have left the meadow lush and full of wildflowers. In a small depression in the earth you come upon a round pool. Its surface is unrippled, and as you look into it, you see your own face... You rest by the pool, considering. You remember all of those people you have most admired. Looking into the pool was like watching a film of your own life: your childhood, family, friends, most important relationships and achievements. You ponder these, feeling the whole of your life up until this moment. Although you have had many different experiences, you see that all of them have led you to this place where you are now. Taking a breath, you glance across the bright meadow toward the edge of the wood, the trees' leaves shining in the sun like an emerald necklace. Slowly, you rise...

Part II

Creative
Dream Themes:
Into the Woods

Two roads diverged in a yellow wood,
And sorry I could not travel both
And be one traveler, long I stood
And looked down one as far as I could
To where it bent in the undergrowth,

Then took the other, as just as fair,
And having perhaps the better claim,
Because it was grassy and wanted wear,
Though as for that the passing there
Had worn them really about the same,

And both that morning equally lay
In leaves no step had trodden black.
Oh, I kept the first for another day!
Yet knowing how way leads on to way,
I doubted if I should ever come back.

I shall be telling this with a sigh
Somewhere ages and ages hence:
Two roads diverged in a wood, and I—
I took the one less traveled by,
And that has made all the difference.

—Robert Frost, *The Road Not Taken*[53]

Chapter 4

Dreaming and the Creative Process

I dream of a very tall building. It's in the process of being built and there are scaffolds and steps. It looks sort of like the inside of the Arc de Triomphe. I'm climbing it with alacrity and joy and laughter. Quite often it's day but it's not very bright because I'm inside the structure going up. I have no sense of dizziness or discomfort or vertigo. I'm just climbing. I can't tell you how delicious that is!

—Maya Angelou[54]

MAYA ANGELOU HAS DREAMED this dream for the past twenty years. She sees a connection between it and her writing going well. It may represent the feeling of writing for her at such times: in a foreign land, triumphant, victorious, and as if she is creating a structure inside of a new place within as she writes. Her creative process is represented in her dream.

The processes of dreaming and of creativity are similar, and both are unlike the way we think in ordinary waking life. If we can begin to trust the workings of our natural dream language, it can aid us in developing our creativity. Our dreams will become our art.[55]

In this chapter, we explore how dreams and creativity are similar and what blended dream images might mean. Then, we will see how some well-known creative people's dreams inspired them to solve creative problems and produce some of their best work.

Primary Process: The Language of Dreaming and Creativity

The first red spot on a white canvas may at once
suggest to me the meaning of "morning redness,"
and from there I dream further with my color.

—Hans Hofmann

Dreams reflect a form of thinking that is beyond our conscious control. The dream language is similar to the way we made sense of the world before we learned to speak—through image and metaphor. It mimics the way we think when we create. Freud called this kind of thinking *primary process*, and believed it was essential for any kind of creative work. Primary process is unconstrained by logic and is based on the way we associate one idea or image with another. Its strange, illogical sequences of images fill our creating minds.

Surrealist painter Max Ernst gives an example of the way the dream language works during a creative act:

A complete, real thing, with a simple function apparently fixed... (an umbrella), coming suddenly into the presence of another real thing, very different and no less incongruous (a sewing machine) in surroundings where both must feel out of place (on a dissecting table), escapes by this very fact from its simple function and its own identity; through a new relationship its false absolute will be transformed into a different absolute, at once true and poetic: the umbrella and the sewing machine will make love...[this is a] pairing of two realities which apparently cannot be paired on a plane apparently not suited to them.[56]

This type of thinking is essential when creating, whether awake or while dreaming: ordinary conscious thinking is simply too concerned with time sequence and with things as we are used to seeing them to provide the original connections we need.

Exercise: Rearranging Dream Images

As Max Ernst wrote, using the images of umbrella, table, and sewing machine, creative acts pair "two realities which apparently cannot be paired on a plane apparently not suited to them." Dreams, our nightly creative acts, do so as well.

For this exercise, try writing down in random order all the images from a recent vivid and memorable dream. Now, set a timer for ten or fifteen minutes, and as fast as you can, write a new story using all the images. (Time pressure helps you disconnect your intellectual, thinking mind and let your creativity flow!)

I used this exercise for my dissertation research, and found that the way you use those images in a waking story is similar to how you do so in dreams. Each night, you receive a font of inspirational images that can be transformed into many different tales, each uniquely your own.

If you are not in the mood to write, you can do this exercise artistically. Set a timer, again, and paint or draw the images without thinking too much about them. You might be surprised at which images you pair with which, and how the whole composition presents itself. In turn, those connections might give you insight into the meaning of the original dream images.

The Process of Dreaming: Blended Images

You can observe primary process at work in dreams, where strange shifts of time and space and unusual transformations of image and meaning fill your dreaming mind. Biologists and cognitive psychologists find that our distorted dream images mirror the perfectly normal, associative process we use every day to interpret our experiences and integrate them with our memories.[57] In other words, we all think creatively to some degree all of the time.

When awake, this process is automatic: we do not know we are thinking by association. As Jung wrote, "It is on the whole probable that we continually dream, but that consciousness makes such a noise that we do not hear it."

You have the chance to make use of this form of unconstrained thinking when you create. Ernst's sewing machine and umbrella making love is a dream language image. It could not occur in waking life; it is illogical, and it is original. The meeting of two things that have never met before, be they ideas, images, or words, is the essence of creativity. Things that do not go together in the waking world often meet and blend in our dreams. This is called *condensation,* and it is one of the characteristics of dream language that we use while creating, too.[58]

A mechanism of dreams first observed by Freud, condensation is the production of an image that represents the melding of separate ideas that are closely associated with one another in our memories. The ideas being blended are linked by feeling, sharing a common emotional tone in our minds.

In chapter 2, we looked at the importance of dream emotions. Look closely at the feelings your blended dream images evoke: how do you feel about these things or people when you are awake? Because they are blended in dreams, you probably have similar feelings about both of them, although you may not previously have realized it.

For example, the most common images to be melded in dreams are those of two people we know—either the two become one ("she was both my sister and my business partner") or they alternate ("first he was my best friend, then he turned into my son"). The blended images of the first dreamer's sister and business partner indicate that they are somehow linked in her mind. The best friend and son of the second dreamer are also associated. The results, sister equals business partner and best friend equals son, contain the truth of the emotional connections between the dreamers and those other people. How are the dreamer's feelings about his son like those for his best friend? Is he parenting his friend in some way? Does the business partner feel as close as a sister? Closer, perhaps, than is comfortable? If so, the dreamer might want to take action by talking to her business partner or further exploring her feelings in another way.

Blended dream images can also represent parts of the dreamer's psyche that are becoming integrated, or whole, within. We dream of these inner figures as if they were other people who are relatively known or unknown, in accordance with how well we know the parts of ourselves represented by the dream figures. (Sometimes, this joining is represented in our dreams as sexuality, as we discovered in chapter 10.) For instance, a forty-eight-year-old poet named Charles told me the following dream:

> I dreamed I was back in my college poetry class, studying for a poetry test, but reading all of these engineering books for some reason. The teacher, who I'll call Dr. X (she really was my teacher in college), looked very old. She was passing out some kind of test. It was just a sheet of paper with some trees on it. I looked up at her, trying to figure out what she wanted of me, but she changed into Emily Dickinson. She had bits of leaves and grass stuck to her clothes. She just smiled and nodded her head, sharply, just once.

At first, Charles was mystified: Grass? Emily Dickinson? Engineering? Then, he focused on the metamorphosis of Dr. X into Emily Dickinson, searching for a common feeling tone.

"Well, I admire them both. I always thought of Dr. X as being locked up in that academic thing, you know. A poet in academia—

I don't know how she was able to express herself in all that bureaucratic structure. I don't know how anyone can. I can't. Emily Dickinson. Her work is just simple. Her poems are eloquent, they don't put on any airs."

I thought about how Dr. X had become Emily Dickinson and wondered whether Charles had experienced (or needed to experience) a similar transformation. Had he gone, or did he wish to go, from being an academically minded poet to someone more "simple" and natural?

Charles volunteered that he had been struggling with the form of his work. It was hard for him to take himself seriously as a poet, and in order to give himself some credibility, he had been trying to be a "good poet." To Charles, that meant reading endless books on poetic form and structure: meter, rhyme, and rhythm. Just prior to the dream, he had been working on a sonnet.

Now the dream made more sense. After we talked about it some more, Charles summarized what we had discovered:

> Lately, I am in a classroom. Rather than just writing down what I see and feel, the way Emily Dickinson would, or the way I'd really like to, I'm studying poetry, doing the same ridiculous thing Dr. X would want me to do as an academic. These books I'm reading—I'm trying to engineer a poem. That will never work!

The dream showed Charles that his test or challenge was to become more natural and to use nature in his work, which may well lead him to be a more successful poet. Charles and I had been working on his difficulty accepting his calling to be a poet. Poetry was part of him. And he needed to accept that his work was valuable and

worthwhile. The dream taught him that he has a strong internal figure (Dr. X) who expects him to write in a certain way and does not
allow him to create his best work. Dr. X has been there a long time
(she is "old") and, as the "head of the class," has a lot of intellectual
power over Charles.[59] Now that he has an image of Dr. X, he can
begin to challenge her proclamations. Charles also has a more supportive inner figure, who encourages him to write in the way he
would most like to, helping him to stand up to Dr. X. The dream
represents Charles's growing acquaintance with the critical and supportive parts of himself, suggesting that the two parts (Dr. X and
Emily Dickinson; intellect and feeling) may soon join to help him
create his own *Leaves of Grass.*

Our dreams represent inner connections by creatively forming from two ideas or images an image that is both and neither.
When creating, we give form to these blended meanings in our
work. The ability to combine many layers of meaning into a single
image is a precious creative skill we often use in our dreams.

Dream language not only mirrors our waking psychic processes
the way we practice our crafts, suspending our logical mind to produce more unusual creations, but it can also point to emotional
links that turn up as themes in our creative work and that we might
explore more fully, or of which we might want to break free.

The Process of Creating

When you create by allowing your mind to relax, lessening conscious control over your thoughts, original images burst forth. This
process then reverses itself, and consciousness resumes control,

synthesizing whatever has appeared to produce your creative work. This is exactly what happens when you go to sleep and dream, then awaken and consciously recall your dreams, and this may be why researchers have found a relationship between the fluidity of waking thought and symbolism in dreams.[60]

Remember from chapter 3 that people who create do not necessarily have more bizarre elements in their dreams than do others. They are, however, better able to make what they do have more meaningful by transforming it and communicating it to others. They are poised to make use of their inspirational dream material in their creative lives.

Dreams as Creative Inspiration

The greatest writers, poets, and artists confirm the fact that their work comes to them from beyond the threshold of consciousness.
—*Percy Bysshe Shelley*

Drama is what you do when you have a dream while you're awake.
—*Ron Smothermon*

The notion that it is possible to receive creative ideas from dreams has become part of our culture. European romanticists, Dadaists, and surrealists all used images that originated in their dreams. The composer Tartini dreamed of the devil playing a music piece, which Tartini transcribed upon waking and named "The Devil's Trill Sonata." Beethoven and Mozart heard portions of music in their dreams, which they would transcribe upon waking. Such writers as John Keats, Robert Louis Stevenson, Mary Shelley, and William

Blake also reported using dreams for inspiration, as did E. M. Forster, C. S. Lewis, and Anne Sexton. Sculptor Jonathan Borofsky created a giant ruby based on a dream image, and it now hangs inside the Basel branch of the Swiss Bank. Chris Burden, a performance artist, translated a particularly frightening dream into one of his pieces.

In a Lifetime documentary, Anne Rice, author of a number of best-selling novels including her famed vampire series, described how she dreamed of an important fixture in *The Witching Hour* series. Before beginning to write the book, she repeatedly dreamed of a great house. Although she was in California at the time, the dream building was a green plantation house in New Orleans' Garden District, where she imagined all the family would come. She described it as a place with a history, where many souls dwelled. Anyone who has read *The Witching Hour* recognizes this house, and remembers that one of the main characters, Michael Curry, recurrently dreams of it.

Robert Louis Stevenson frequently used his dreams as material for his fiction. He based his Dr. Jekyll and Mr. Hyde on a dream in which he saw a respectable British gentleman transform into a grotesque monster:

> For two days I went about wracking my brains for a plot of any sort; and on the second night I dreamed the scene at the window, and a scene afterward split in two, in which Hyde, pursued for some crime, took the powder and underwent the change in the presence of his pursuers.[61]

In her introduction to *Frankenstein,* Mary Shelley described the creature as he first appeared to her when she was in a dreamlike state:

> I saw the pale student of unhallowed arts kneeling beside the thing he had put together. I saw the hideous phantasm of a man stretched out, and then, on the working of some powerful engine, show signs of life, and stir with an uneasy, half vital motion.[62]

In 1788, William Blake struggled over how to publish his *Songs of Innocence, Songs of Experience* and color illustrations. He dreamed of a man who directed him to publish his *Songs* together, as a series of poems and writings illustrated by colored plates, which, of course, he did.[63]

When Isabel Allende was struggling with the ending of her first novel, *The House of the Spirits,* she dreamed of telling her black-clad grandfather the book's story. When she woke up, she became aware that she had really been telling the story to him all during the writing of the book. That realization helped her write the epilogue.[64]

Dreams help solve creative problems, and they are also used as subject matter. Yeats frequently used his dreams in his creative life. He and his friend, Dorothy Wellesley, exchanged dreams and mused about their possible meanings. In one letter, she wrote to Yeats about a dream in which they were

> . . . in a deep glade surrounded by tall straight full-grown beech trees. You said: "I can fell that tree with a pen-knife." I said: "Then fell that one and prove it." You walked up the slope of the glade. I could just see you making shallow cuts on the bark with your little knife. I

heard Hilda call: "Stand back, stand back." "No," I replied, "it will fall precisely where it wills." It did, I knew this was magic, said to you: "Will you do it again?" You did it again. I said: "Three times it must be done for you are a magician."[65]

Dorothy Wellesley dreams Yeats is using a "penknife," and this image is not lost on Yeats, who replied, referring to his poetry, "I certainly have always felt that I am cutting trees down with a razor or trying to but it takes a dream to make it true."[66]

Other famous creative artists also use their dreams. Filmmaker Orson Welles confided, "Anything I could think up in my dreams, I attempted to photograph." Norman Mailer noted the connection between film and dreaming when he wrote, "Film, at its most compelling, lives in our mind somewhere between our memories and our dreams."

Not only artists and writers, but prominent scientists are also inspired by their dreams: Kukule's famous dream of a coiled snake led to his discovery of the ringed structure of the benzene molecule; Hermann von Helmholtz believed he frequently received answers to his problems through dreams; and Niels Bohr dreamed of what was to become his atom model.

Sifting through dreams for creative ideas takes attention. Several years ago, I was in charge of organizing an international conference on dreams. Each participant was to receive a binder that contained all kinds of information about conference happenings, the local area, and so on. I wanted to paint an evocative image that could be placed at the front of the binder. Finally, after weeks of considering, I had the following dream:

I am walking through a clearing on a sloping hill. The setting seems familiar, and then I realize it is Oxford. There is a glittering lake in front of me and as I look up, I see a sort of castle white with an Italian tile roof. The place is surrounded by trees. It is so beautiful and so peaceful, I am mesmerized by the whole scene.

Gingerly dusting off my brushes, I painted the scene as I had dreamed it. Only later did I realize that the dream castle image was more than it had seemed. The conference site was on a hill, and it was originally designed to mimic the style of Oxford University. The college where the participants were to live was white stucco with adobe-tiled roofs, surrounded by trees. It overlooked the ocean, not a lake. And although it was by no means a castle, it was a university campus, an "ivory tower." With a few primary process transformations, the dream presented an ivory tower removed from the normal world for a time, in close proximity to feeling (water) and the deep wood (unconscious). It was exactly what I hoped the conference would be like for those who participated.[67]

Exercise: Our Own Inspiring Dreams

> Dreaming is an act of pure imagination, attesting in all men
> a creative power, which, if it were available in waking,
> would make every man a Dante or Shakespeare.
>
> —H. F. Hedge

Dreams provide inspiration for all sorts of people. If you would like to be creatively enriched, try this little experiment before going to bed tonight.

First, make sure you have your dream journal beside your bed with an inspiring writing instrument close at hand. Do some relaxing activity (pleasure reading, drawing) just before bed, then write tomorrow morning's date in your journal. Just before dropping off to sleep, imagine yourself waking up in the morning and writing down a dream. Relax and tell yourself several times, "Tonight I will have an inspiring dream."

In the morning, go over the dream in your mind several times before opening your eyes (remember how quickly dreams disappear once the stimulation of the waking world beams in). Then, write the dream down in your journal, quickly underlining words, phrases, and images that immediately strike you. Keep writing quickly; this phase should be completed without much thought.

Leave your dream journal alone for a few days, and let your thoughts concern themselves with other things. When you are ready to create, visit your dream again. At this point, you have several options:

- You can draw or paint the images in the dream exactly as they occurred, or you can let your hand transform the images at will as you re-create them. What do they stir in you? Remind you of?

- You can use the phrases and words you underlined in a new story that has nothing to do with the story of your dream. If you tend to think a lot while writing, you might try setting a timer for two or three minutes, and then aim to use every underlined passage in your story. Time pressure can work wonders at suspending the loud and relentless internal critic.

- Dance the dream. Be a "body impressionist," putting dream feelings and interactions into movement, and see what else appears inside of you.

- Use your dream phrases in a poem, a sort of dream haiku, no matter how silly it ends up sounding. You may have the core of an exceptional piece there.

- Create a photo montage of your dream. Search around your town for views that capture the images of your dream. Make yourself a dream pictorial. What is it about, really?

- Act out the story of your dream as if it were that play you want to write or star in—do a one-person show, or lasso in a few friends for fun. Create new endings, or even new characters. Have each of the characters describe how he or she or it feels the "play" should progress.

To get the most benefit from this exercise, choose something you would ordinarily not do (if you are a writer, dance; if you are an actor, paint or draw). This is wonderful for liberating parts of yourself that can stifle you, if neglected too long. Leave your mind behind. . .

You begin to walk through the flowers away from the pool and the group beyond, alone. You hear the children behind you, joyful in their play, and think back on your own lost childhood. As you make your way through grass that is so tall it reaches your waist, you remember the feeling of being very short, smelling fresh grass and chasing butterflies. Close to the wood now, you know you must soon pass through the portal—a small space beneath two arching tree trunks, overhung with vines, and marked by the ruins of an arch. First, you throw yourself down on your back, breathing in the scents that surround you. Looking up at the sky, you search for shapes in the clouds. . .

Chapter 5

The Theme of Children

The best thoughts you have are when you're young,
and the best you can do is never give up those thoughts.
—Rockwell Kent

NOT ONLY ARE OUR DREAMS like stories or paintings, but they are also pieces of theater. Dreams have a narrative structure, beginning with an introduction (or *exposition*), where we learn the problem. Then we witness the ups and downs of the storyline (*peripeteia*), and, finally, the solution (*lysis*). Like theater, dreams also contain actors, stage settings, entrances, exits, conflict, innuendo, climax, and, sometimes, resolution. Other times, lack of resolution is the most troubling part of our dreams. What would have happened if you hadn't woken up? What might you have done differently, had you been able to dream it over again?

In this chapter and the two that follow, we explore three key plots or themes in our dreams: children, loss, and obstacles in nature and what they might indicate about us and our creative work. These three themes rarely occur in the dreams of those who do not live a creative life, so when they appear, pay attention.

In working with clients and in researching the dream series of people who wrote down their dreams over several years, I discovered that each of these dream/life themes tends to recur at different points in the creative path or spiral. You will integrate these themes into a larger whole when you continue your journey in the woods in part III. In this and the following two chapters, you will meet each of the themes in its turn. But first, here is a way of imagining that journey.

Three Paths through the Wood

Continue to write down your own dreams, as they will become particularly important once you enter the dark wood of the unconscious. Before you can enter, you must know which path you are setting out upon. The paths through the wood are several, and each of them has its perils. Some go further into the forest, and others skirt just inside the edge. Each one represents a different level of the journey toward expressing yourself as creatively as you can in the world.

Three paths will meet before you at the portal and trail off into the wood. One darts beneath the low-hanging branches of the first trees, leading off to the left. There are sunny splotches on this path, and a suspension bridge connects it with the valley clearing down in the center of the forest. This is the outward path. Another path, the inward path, makes its way into the heart of the forest, becoming almost obscured in the cold darkness, and then reemerging in the clearing. The third, the middle path, is circular, traveling up and down small hills from which you will be able to see far into the distance, now descending into the forest, now rising into the sunlight, slowly spiraling down into the valley clearing. These paths will be mentioned at different points throughout the rest of the book. We each have our own way of looking at things, including our dreams. Some like to take what is there exactly as it seems (the outward path), and others like to look for hidden meanings (the inward and middle paths).

When on the outward path, you tend to look for things and people in your real life to explain your dreams: you dreamed of arguing with Sam because you are angry with him, for example. On the inward path, you see dream elements as representing parts of your own self: your dream of arguing with Sam expresses a conflict between two sides of *yourself*, influencing you in opposing ways. The middle path integrates the other two: you are angry with the part of yourself that is similar to, or represented by, Sam. As you walk upon it, you look to your real life in the waking world as well as to your inner needs and conflicts.

These paths are each creative roads and they will all lead to the same place. Consider your own personality before making your choice. The first path is the least treacherous, the second the most perilous, and the third provides balance on the journey. None of the paths is necessarily better than any other; they just offer different ways of looking at dreams.

As you travel through the next two parts of the book, keep in mind that the creative path is both a labyrinth and a spiral, with the same difficulties and challenges appearing again and again throughout our lives and in our dreams. Creativity is cyclic. We all approach and retreat from ourselves and our own self-expression. At times, you may feel as though you have only traveled in circles when you have really moved closer to yourself and to the central clear space in the heart of the wood. Your dreams are way-finders when you are lost, letting you know where you are on your own path, reminding you of how far you have come, and where you have yet to travel.

Now, imagine yourself at the portal. Look carefully at each of the paths, and when you have chosen one, set out upon it. Fully imagine your first few steps into the wood. . .

Dreams of Children

I dream I am with a group of people in a building. Perhaps we are spies. One, a man, is piecing clues together. I help. There are many pieces of paper. A baby is the key. A baby will be born. He finishes piecing the papers together: it is a picture of me as a baby. We discover that on another planet there is virtual reality, and someone is coming here from there. It is the baby, but it is also me.

Maria, a photographer, explained that within this dream, knowing that a baby was coming to earth who was somehow also herself was extremely important, "perhaps the most important thing I've ever known." The dream might lead you to the conclusion that this woman is considering having a child, but this was not the case for

Maria, who had suffered an illness in her twenties that left her unable to conceive. She had never wanted children, and I felt that she was genuinely at peace with her circumstances, rather than denying her true feelings. What struck Maria the most about the dream, besides the feeling of its importance, was the image of the baby as simultaneously being herself and journeying to her from a place that was "virtually real."

I asked her what she thought of being a spy in the dream.

"It's what I do as a photographer," she replied.

There was a connection between her dream and her craft. Maria had been in therapy for several months, suffering from burnout. Although it was not obvious to her, concerned friends repeatedly told her that she seemed overstressed and preoccupied. She drove herself quite hard, kept long hours, and admitted that she was a perfectionist. When asked what she did for fun, Maria was stumped. Her photography studio had become a place of labor, not love. Maria's dream heralded a rejuvenating time. As she began to loosen the adult bonds of expectation she had placed upon her work and began to play with her photography, her energy returned. Along the way, Maria began to photograph children so that she would not again forget the importance of being childlike. For people like Maria, who disregard their playful impulses as immature and at odds with their desire to be successful, such dreams can be crucial if we pay attention to their meaning.

Dreams about children can reveal the importance of your own childlike and playful qualities. Such dreams can communicate the ways in which you treat your own vulnerable self and the impact that treatment may have on your life.

Rachel, a painter, overcomes danger and fear in this part of a longer dream:

> I am looking out a window at a cave that is formed by sand that has mounded up from the beach. If you look out the window from the second floor, you can see the cave and beyond, the ocean. While I'm looking out at the cave, I'm also climbing in the cave. The colors are gold and blue—dazzling. But as I look at the cave, my sister/friend's mother appears next to me. She is screaming at my sister/friend to stop climbing in the cave because it's dangerous. Then the girl in the cave becomes me and the climbing is a great feeling.

Rachel's dream contains several elements we explored in previous chapters: water, up and down, blended imagines. The child in the dream actually becomes the dreamer. Rachel is both an exploring child and herself. She does not allow fear or danger to stop her, and she is rewarded with happiness.

Thea, who recently entered college as a dance major after several years of performing, illustrates her willingness to communicate with her own childlike self:

> I am with a little girl I used to know in the dream, but have never seen before in real life. She's dancing around outside and wants to be a successful dancer, but she is afraid it won't happen. She doesn't know how to be. I tell her not to worry, she has lots of time. At first, I fear she'll cling to me, but I quickly like her as I get to know her again. She's a little pistol! She fears I will go off again now and I say I will come visit her.

Entering college, Thea is in danger of neglecting her spontaneous, nonrational side and becoming overly intellectual and "adult" in her approach to dance. Although the dream seems to express this concern, Thea reassures her child-self.

In our dreams of children, we inevitably encounter long-ago scenes and feelings that may be painful. These feelings also reach out to us in our "fictional" characters, in the look of the blossoms we are painting, or in our own expression in a photograph like Maria's. While looking at the face of our business partner, we remember how we felt when we saw our grandfather's angry eyes; or we experience the feeling of eternal hopelessness when no one seems to want what we have made: "I will never succeed!" Dreaming, we feel again the forgotten frustration. We cry tears from long ago that have remained housed in our bodies, daring to peer out of our watery eyes only in the land of our dreams.

As children, we saw, heard, and learned things about those we loved that we were not supposed to know. These are the things we must communicate somehow, how those experiences affected us and what they meant. Our pasts affect what we choose to produce as adults. We may find ourselves repeating the same patterns in our work and personal lives that we grew up with in our families. Those patterns seep into our creative process and into our dreams.

Creativity requires strength and, occasionally, the courage to open oneself up to look inside at our hurt places. Isolation is necessary for creation, yet all of that time spent alone is bound to act as a mirror. One can push away troubling thoughts and feelings in the peopled world, but alone, can be besieged, especially when trying to work. We mine the depths of our lives for the substance of our creations; what some of us are after is the truth of our own lives. We want to know what the truth is, and we want other people to know we know it, to recognize it themselves, and to be moved by it. Our dreams reveal what we wish to communicate. The deeper we go, the more universal and true the territory. The farther we journey, the more we move from the outward to the inward path, and eventually arrive in the middle.

As a person who creates, feelings, thoughts, dreams, memories, and skills are all you have to work with. You are alone with your blank canvas, page, screen, stage, or script, and what you place there, your own truth, is to be honored. Your dreams of children lay you before yourself afresh and offer you the chance to reclaim what gifts you've put aside, which bring with them a revitalization of creative energy when rediscovered. They also give you an opportunity to honor what you produce with the exploring child you hold within.

Children and the Creative Process

Dreams that feature children may also describe your creative process and give some hints about your future creative work. For instance, Maurice Sendak, who in chapter 3 described the creative process as similar to the birth process, had dreams of someone trying to take his child away during the period just before he delivered a manuscript to his publisher.

I have had similar dreams, such as the following, which woke me up the night after I signed the contract to write this book:

> I am with a man, a stranger. He is concerned and wants to help me. In the dream, I want to have a child. He tells me it must happen this year, or it will be too late. Then, he counts off the months. He's going to help it happen, but not physically, for in the dream I am already pregnant. He says I will carry the child through the winter and it will be delivered in the spring. By Christmas, it will be old enough to interact, so I can carry it around and introduce it to people.

I was not thinking about motherhood at that time. But I was pregnant with the book; the contract called for it to be completed in the spring and published in late autumn!

Yeats's correspondence contains some compelling dreams with children in them. In the continuation of Dorothy Wellesley's dream described in the last chapter, the dreamer tries to tell a group of people that Yeats had indeed performed a magical act by felling the trees. They do not believe her:

> Suddenly before me stood a small child. A little girl with long dark hair, a bright colour, a small pointed chin most marked and with eyes of luminous emerald. I turned to the group of people and said: "This is the child of Yeats." Fear crept on me, and I could feel that people were afraid also. So to prevent fear gaining on me and on them I put out my hand and held that of the child, saying: "You see she is true, she is real, for I can touch her."[68]

The dreamer's interaction with Yeats produced a new creative child whom Wellesley is ready to introduce to others.

Children Exploring the World

When creating, you may expect to dream of children who seem to be seeking something and exploring the natural world. This makes sense: those who create are seekers after the truth, and children are natural seekers, exploring the world with the freshness of spring. Everything is new to a child, as it is to our creative minds, which behave like little children who come across something for the first time. Their fleeting look of open-mouthed awe is replaced by a tentative smile before they burst into joy, eyes springing open with delight. They reach for the object, turn it over and toss it about. Children who come upon something new are all eyes and fingers and feeling.

In order to create, it helps to revisit that time. When you begin a project, approach what is ahead with a childlike, dazed wonder. Willing to explore all potential alleys of adventure, you must not censor any possibility or idea in the beginning. If you can let your thoughts and feelings flow, observing them as if you were a child with a new toy, you can gain the attitude of newness and enthusiasm so important for the beginning of any creative venture. Yet, childhood was long ago and it can be difficult to remember what it felt like to be a child. Your dreams of children can remind you of how to let go of your adult ways.

In your journal, you may find dreams about unfamiliar children who seem to be exploring. Do not be surprised if these dreams tend to occur when you are embarking upon new projects. When beginning your creative work, you are most awake to inspiration, as you look within yourself and in the outside world for new ideas. Many believe that what we create represents the struggles we are having with ourselves. In our musings at the beginning of a creative work, we scour the landscape of the soul for what is coming within. We change ourselves by bringing out into the world what is inside.

Children in dreams are auspicious. They may represent a new part of the psyche, just beginning to be recognized and expressed.[69] Dream children mirror inner rebirth, as in Maria's dream, where a new part of herself, a potentially playful and renewed child, was to be born. To the inner child, all is new and as yet unexplored.

Children in dreams also appear in therapy when the dreamer has broken through a complex pattern or is becoming emotionally aware of an old way of being.[70] This awareness releases tension and can lead to an explosion of creativity. The child, who is at the beginning of life, represents the new awareness, also at its beginning.[71]

One of my clients, Brandon, an interior designer, dreams about a child during creative times:

> A few nights ago I dreamed I was with a little kid again. He looks familiar, probably from other dreams. He's a cute little guy. He half leads, half follows me. We're walking through tall grass and trees and he just can't get enough of it all. He picks things up off the ground, smells them, throws it all up in the air, runs circles around me. Pretty soon there's just this scattered bunch of leaves and twigs and pinecones and other strange objects all over the place. So disorganized! The complete opposite of how I prefer to work. But he loved it! Maybe I should try it. Loosen up a little bit.

When you are able to release your adult way of being and open yourself up to creative ideas, they rise from deep within, and you receive them with a special emotional intensity. We plant the seed and check the soil for signs of sprouting. If we can avoid tugging on the new shoots and watch with the reverence and awe of a child, we will be rewarded with fresh growth blossoming into a new creative work.

Small children do not begin exploring a new thing by asking "why" or "what" questions. They make statements to themselves: *This is a Thing. Look at this Thing!* They touch it instead of analyzing it. So, too, might we touch our ideas, feel them, and move them around, rather than dissecting them, criticizing them, and watching them vaporize.

We adults are bombarded with messages about acting our age, being professional, successful, and mature. It may be hard for us to approach our new ideas with the freedom of a five-year-old, as it was for Maria, the photographer, in her craft-become-business.

Dreams hear no such messages, and it is easy to view our dreams with childlike awe or downright confusion: *What was THAT? Did I make THAT in my own head?*

☐ ≈≈ ☐ ≈≈ ☐ ≈≈ ☐ ≈≈ ☐ ≈≈ ☐ ≈≈ ☐ ≈≈ ☐ ≈≈ ☐ ≈≈ ☐

Exercise: Awakening Childlike Wonder

You can experience a childlike feeling by waking each morning with the intention to quietly recall your dreams, and then let your mind touch and play with them a bit before getting up. Wonder at your own imagination. What a glorious thing, to be able to create a world every night!

And what a strange world it was, too... *Look at those funny little miniature trees!* When you go to begin your creative project, take this feeling with you. There is no reason why your new venture should be begun with deep, intellectual musings or heavy and serious consideration. There will be time enough for practical concerns later. In the beginning, vitality is everything. Approach your creative thoughts as if you were meeting them for the first time, playfully. Greet each one with open arms, no matter how foolish, as if you were embracing an errant child. Let the idea emerge. Have a rubber band close by to snap yourself with, or a little bell to ring, when you begin to slip back into adult thought. Keep your dream journal near and when you find yourself becoming too serious, read a few lines with your child eyes.

Children in Danger

Those who seek may run into trouble. We begin by seeking; danger can come later when we stumble upon something about ourselves we did not know before. Creativity is often painful work, especially for those who choose the inward path. It requires the ability to touch places in oneself that are scarred, freshly healed, or even still-open wounds. As one actor client vividly put it, we stick our hands into our sides and pull out our own guts to feed our creative monster. This is not true of everyone (what is?), but remember that many famous creative people's lives hold stores of childhood suffering, adult isolation, and even depression. Their best work can come following the descent into the dangerous depths of their pasts, still present in the psyche, as if those experiences were still happening every day, right now.

As joyful as our creative lives make us, fear, despair, and feelings of isolation and loss are part of moving through life creatively, no matter which path we choose. Unpleasant feelings can flood through us and our dreams during the spiraling creative journey. One of the dream plots in which apprehension arises is when we dream of children in danger. Such a dream can indicate several different things about the dreamer, and you should consider each of them before deciding about the meaning of such a dream.

First, from an outward path perspective, endangered children in dreams may represent real experiences of children we know or experiences we might have had in childhood. Although those experiences are years and years past, they live on in memory, visiting in dreams whenever a current situation sparks an old feeling.

Childhood danger is rarely expressed directly in dreams as the dreamer's being attacked as a child, though, and when it is, it is usually only after much self-exploration or therapy. More often, we observe other children being hurt. For instance, women who were sexually abused as children often dream more often than others of unfamiliar children being pursued and attacked.[72]

Childhood experiences are also often metaphorically represented in dreams, as in this one from Manuel, a successful, forty-eight-year-old entrepreneur at a crossroads in his career as well as in his dream:

> I am standing at an intersection. I see a bunch of kids
> waiting to cross at the light, as if they were outside of a

school or something. They are little kids. For some reason, I feel somewhat worried about them. As the light changes to green, I hear a car shrieking—that's the only word I can use for the sound—and it comes barreling down the road. I can see it will not stop. It will hit the kids. I am horrified and start screaming, trying to do something, but too far away to do anything but watch. I want to call the ambulance. I see the driver just as one boy is hit. He looks familiar. Perhaps it is my father, but no, it couldn't be, I think. My father is dead.

Manuel suffered physical abuse at the hands of his father, who hit him repeatedly and mercilessly throughout his childhood, occasionally sending him to the hospital. His father would become enraged and shout at Manuel in a high-pitched voice, much like the shrieking in the dream. The week before having this dream, Manuel confided in a flat voice, "It was impossible to get out of his way. He would just run over us." This dream helped Manuel to emotionally remember his abuse. Rather than being able to recall only the pictures he could never forget, Manuel now had the feelings to accompany them. As a result, Manuel was able to reexperience himself as a child being abused and, after time, to let go of the self-image of a still-abused and victimized child. Manuel was able to recognize that the fear and horror expressed in the dream had been with him all of his life, even though he had not been aware of them. The dream represented the beginning of a long process of recovering his childhood, moving on, and becoming an assertive adult who can create without horror.

Along with replaying and confronting us with real feelings we felt in childhood, on the inward path endangered dream children represent us. The child within accompanies us throughout our lives and can be heard the loudest in those who were emotionally wounded. The child we were and still are needs our attention, respect, and caring. Again, he or she also needs our willingness to be childlike, because the child can help us find our creativity.

An endangered dream child is unprotected and vulnerable. He or she may be chased by others (or even the dreamer) with cruel intent, or something in the environment may try to harm the child. Whichever it is, the dreamer notes the child is in danger and usually feels apprehensive about it. Such a dream might translate as: "I am feeling vulnerable in this dangerous adult world. I need protection from people who might hurt me."

It is easy to see how this relates to our creativity. Because our dreams represent aspects of ourselves and children represent our creativity, endangered dream children indicate that our creativity *is right now* in danger of being destroyed or hurt. Sometimes that danger comes from other people in our dreams. But those "other people" are also parts of us—we created them. We need to ask ourselves whether we are chipping away at our own creative lives.

This fragment of a longer dream from Emily illustrates that she must take action to protect what is new within her, her vulnerable creativity:

> This woman came in with a little girl of about three. She didn't pay much attention to the little girl and the girl picked up a toy and ran out of the store. I chased her out to the street and she ran in front of a car that almost hit her. I finally caught up with her and brought her back to the store and yelled at her mother for being so careless.

Here is another example of a mother endangering a child. Rebecca, a successful pianist, shared this telling dream with me:

> I just had a baby girl. She was very tiny and beautiful. I was surprised at how warmly I felt toward her and how much love I had for her. My mother was there. The baby was very fragile; wasn't getting enough blood or something. Later, my mother had been taking care of her—no, watching her—and had left her in the car with the windows rolled up. It was very hot and I knew she would die. My mother couldn't remember where she'd left the car. I couldn't believe her incompetence! I was furious!

Rebecca struggled with periods of "creative avoidance": the desire to do her creative work, but a feeling of great anxiety when confronted with the space and time in which to begin. This left her frustrated and tired from struggling with the ambivalence. As she was growing up, Rebecca participated in this same struggle, but then it was an external one: her mother both supported and devalued her music.

"She really loved to hear me play, and she would reward me with a treat or a trip or something of that nature whenever I had done particularly well. But she also seemed to really need me around. She was a lonely person, didn't have many friends. I came home every day to practice for several hours, and she would always just sit or stand there, trying to find a reason to interrupt me. You know, 'Rebecca, look at what the dog is doing!' or even worse, 'You can practice later.'"

When I asked Rebecca how she felt while practicing with her mother as a constant companion, she squirmed.

"Music is a private thing. I loved my mother, but I wanted to be alone with it."

A few sentences later, Rebecca described the feeling of her mother's devouring interest in her work as "suffocating." Rebecca tried to look at her dream self and dream mother as representing two sides of her own self that simultaneously love her to play and then try to divert her.

"I don't try to divert myself. I just get so nervous, so restless. At first it's as if I'm saying, 'All I want to do is play!' and then, 'All I want to do is anything but this!'...It's exactly what I felt like when I was on the way home from school. I couldn't wait to get my hands on the keys. But once I was there, with my mother tromping about the place, I just wanted to be AWAY."

Rebecca's relationship with her mother was impeding her life as a pianist, even though her mother had died years before. Her nervousness was more than the memory of an old situation with her mother; it was also a symptom of a deeper fear of being consumed by and becoming a servant to the too-great needs of her mother. The dream helped Rebecca eventually see that what is without is also within, and to turn her focus in therapy and in her work from her mother to herself. Rebecca realized that although her mother was gone, she had unconsciously adopted her mother's behavior toward her own creativity.

Rebecca was able to gain control over her creative process by imagining her dream mother every time she sat down to play and felt nervous. We developed a ritual where Rebecca would imagine her mother, recall the dream, and then say out loud, "Open the window, mother. The baby's suffocating!" Then she would imagine the baby pink and invigorated, growing rapidly into herself as an adult. At the end of her practice sessions, she would imagine her mother entering the room from the garden to let her know how lovely her playing sounded.

From the outward path perspective, Rebecca's real mother neglected and thwarted her creativity, as shown in the dream. On the inward path, Rebecca finds an inner "mother" who thwarts her urge to play. Understanding that this inner mother originated with Rebecca's experiences with her real mother requires a middle path view.

In Leo Tolstoy's *Anna Karenina,* when the character Konstantin Levin tries to make a break from his old life, doubts set upon him. Tolstoy eloquently describes Levin's struggle with the past, one Rebecca and so many of us share:

> All these traces of his life seemed to clutch him, and to say to him: "No, you're not going to get away from us, and you're not going to be different, but you're going to be the same as you've always been; with doubts, everlasting dissatisfaction with yourself, vain efforts to amend, and falls, and everlasting expectation, of a happiness which you won't get, and which isn't possible for you."
>
> These the things said to him, but another voice in his heart was telling him that he must not fall under the sway of the past, and that one can do anything with oneself.[73]

You may find yourself surrounded by people who do not respect your creativity, as was Rebecca in childhood. Once you begin to nourish and protect your creativity, you learn to require respect from friends and family. Sometimes people can become annoyed by such requests. They are used to being allowed to distract you, and they do not want to change. However, by asking for what you need (such as emotional space and support for your work), you allow the people you care about to best care for you. You also give them the chance to let you know what they might need from you. There are always threats to the creative life, and some of them are unavoidable. To the greatest extent possible, though, take courage to make your creative expression a priority in your life and fearlessly protect your creative children. If you do not, you may dream of little ones in danger.

As you move toward nurturing the vulnerable parts of yourself and allow your creativity to flow, you may notice your dreams changing, as Lisa did. Following a long series of dreams in which children were in danger, helping her to begin to nurture, protect, and attend to her childlike self and her creativity, Lisa had the following dream:

> I was a young child—I'm not sure if I was male or female—part of a colony of people trying to make it as farmers on another planet. We were living in a large cave, and I looked outside and felt that it had been cloudy but warm for several days, but now that the sun had come out, the frost was back and was killing the young shoots of the plants that had been sown. My father (not my father in reality) tried to reassure me, and himself, by saying the cold would probably not last long and there might be time to plant again, even if all the young plants died. I am not sure if failure with the farming meant starvation or simply a forced return to Earth. Then I was standing on a low hill overlooking the fields, but they seemed autumnal rather than vernal—the grasses were tall and brown, and the sunlight was a toasted sort of yellow. I saw trucks driving into the fields to gather the pumpkins which seemed almost as large as the trucks.

We hoped we could live off of them over the winter if all
else failed; there seemed to be a great abundance.

This dream from Rebecca, which occurred about two years
after the first (of the baby trapped in the car), demonstrates her
changing attitude toward her creative child:

> I dreamed of a little girl, about five years old. She was sit-
> ting on my knee while we somehow played a duet of
> "Scenes from Childhood" by Schumann. She was quite
> good, too! We played on and on. No one else was there.

Exercise: Endangered Children

Here are some questions to ask of your endangered child dreams.
They integrate the outward and inward paths so that you may
arrive at the middle. Write your responses in your dream journal
and watch your dreams change…

- Why am I having this dream now? What's happening in
  my work now that would produce this dream?

- In what ways am I endangering my own creativity?

- Am I treating my own hopes the way they were treated
  by others when I was a child?

- What do I do when I feel myself beginning to soar with
  a new idea? Does this remind me of what happened
  in my dream? In my childhood?

- What does the dream child need? Is there something I can imagine saying to him or her? Doing for him or her?

- What do I need from others in order to create that I'm not getting now? What would happen if I received it?

- What action can I take to ensure I get what I need?

- Imagine you know someone who has difficulty expressing their child side. How would you encourage that person? Now encourage yourself to do those things.

❧❧❧❧❧❧❧❧❧

No one else is on this path you are walking. It dips and curves, and its changes have made it impossible for you to see what awaits you. Your footsteps sound hollow as you walk on a thick layer of decomposing pine needles and leaves that have turned the ground dark and fragrant. Except for the sound of twigs snapping beneath your shoes, it is very quiet. Suddenly, you stop. Was that movement in the trees? Looking about, you sense someone. But the light is dim, with twilight just beginning to cloak the treetops. This is a strange forest; it feels different here somehow. All of your senses are sharp. Could that have been a small creature or a child left alone in the wood, darting by too fast to see? Troubled but curious, you quicken your pace toward a sharp bend in the path. Catching just a glimpse of someone small leaping ahead, you begin to run. A few more turns, and you stop short. The woods are darker, now, almost a thicket. There are several paths converging here. Which way did you come? You are most certainly lost. The forest seems empty. Wolves begin to howl from far off. You gather your cloak about you in search of a warm place to hide for the night. . .

≈ Chapter 6 ≈

The Theme of Loss

IN THE LAST CHAPTER, dreams of children exploring the world and being in danger showed us the importance of being childlike and inquisitive in the early stages of creating a new project. They help us explore our "inner nature" by reminding us of our vulnerability and playfulness, and remind us to value our own creativity and to protect it.

But the things that happen to children in our dreams are happening to *them*, not to us as adults. We have some emotional distance from them in the dream; however, we create all parts of our dreams, so our dream children must be part of ourselves. In our dreams, we are really observing ourselves and our own carefree seeking that may sometimes lead to danger, and we are fed by remembering our own past experiences. But still, the feelings that go along with taking risks are muted when it seems to be others who are risking and not ourselves—more like watching a film than experiencing our own lives.

The next theme in the dreams of people who create that occurs more often than in others' is loss. Loss becomes a theme in our adult dreams, emerging when our childlike nature leads us to reach toward those inner places called up by the creative process, usually when a new project is underway. Every new awareness creates a death of unawareness. We can never go back to the way we were before.

Dream loss also comes in many forms. The most common are losing possessions, losing health through illness or physical or mental problems, and losing a person through death or rejection.

Lost or Defective Possessions

Creative dreamers often lose things or are in danger of losing them. Material possessions can stand for less tangible elements in our lives. Common things dreamers lose include keys, cars, clothes, houses, and body parts. Here are some of their metaphorical equivalents.

Houses

Locks keep us safe inside our own "houses." A house is, metaphorically speaking, the place our minds inhabit. Dream houses provide a pictorial view of the psyche, the structure of our own personalities, which can be "run down," as in this dream from a young journalist who had to clear "tons of junk" from her psyche in order to pursue her career dreams:

> I am in my childhood house. I had moved out. I went
> back to pick up a few things I'd left and needed. I got
> there and there was tons of junk. I started in my room
> and threw most of it away. I didn't need this stuff any-
> more. It was an overwhelming task.

During times of change, our inner dream houses can be in the process of being remodeled or rebuilt. Clients in therapy often have a series of dreams of structures in poor repair that go through demolition and reconstruction.

Rebecca (the pianist) had the following dream after several months during which she practiced the ritual discussed in the last chapter. She had begun to defend her own creative time by telling her friends when she needed uninterrupted time to work, and reserving those times for herself.

> I dreamed I was living in a gorgeous new house. I woke
> up and saw the outside door had come open. I had for-
> gotten to close it. I was afraid someone had come in to
> rob me of something. Someone had, but they hadn't
> taken anything. Everything seemed to be in place.

Rebecca had recently allowed someone to intrude on her practicing time in a way that had been threatening to her. The other person accused her of being selfish and even used Rebecca's mother's magic words: "You can practice later!" Rebecca had gone for a walk with her just to appease her and afterward decided never to do that again. But she had opened the door, and her psyche remembered.

Kevin is an entrepreneur who worked hard to overcome the negative effect on his creativity of early sabotage by his adopted family, and later by acquaintances and friends. His creative process was frequently aborted. He would meet with some success, and then someone from the outside (or he, himself) would sabotage him. After several years of working with his dream material and watching his inner houses change, he had a final dream to represent the threat of sabotage. In this dream, he is close to water and living in a new "house":

> I am living in a place by the ocean. It is peaceful and had been built by this woman and man who had set it up and planted around it. It is big and airy with lots of gazebo structures and such. On the last day before its completion the place begins to transform. An evil witch had cast a spell and an evil man, her assistant, had helped. The man and woman who had built the place, who looked the same as the other pair, but whom I knew to be good, descend in a wooden elevator. They know there is a hole in the magic. They are going to find it and stop the transformation. I join with them. We are going to meet the evil pair face to face. I know we will stop them.

Keys

We use keys in dreams to unlock the interior "doors" to the hidden rooms of the psyche. Keys let us in to all kinds of mysterious and dangerous places. Turning the key in the lock, we enter a new room, a new part of ourselves we may not have known was there.

Aria, a talented poet, dreamed of a key that had long been lost in her dream world. She found it, and discovered it fit the lock to an old trunk, which she was afraid to open. Once she did so, she was confronted with old, long-buried feelings and memories that had been "locked up." She used her discovery to produce a new series of poems.

Vehicles

We may also dream of losing our vehicle, or of having one damaged or defective. We use our cars to "move" from one place to another in our lives. So is the case with our dreams. A car that once worked and now does not may mean that your old way of moving through the world is no longer appropriate to who you have become. Having a damaged car may metaphorically represent your feeling that the ways you used to create have been ruined somehow. You cannot move out of the situation; you're stuck in a useless car. Several artists with whom I have worked dream of their cars suddenly losing power on a hill, or losing their brakes. The car will begin to go backward and the dreamer typically feels afraid and out of control. Such a dream is likely to occur when the dreamer is under extreme stress and is "going backward" in time, using coping strategies that were appropriate when he or she was quite young, but that have outgrown their usefulness in adulthood. Recall that, when creating, we regress in order to produce our works. Dreams may reflect this heading backward in time with a theme of moving backward without control.

The kind of vehicle we use is also important, and vehicles that move across water can be important for those of us who create. Are you skating across the surface of things, are you flooded with feeling and in danger of capsizing, or is a huge wave on the horizon? In the next chapter, we will explore the meaning of natural obstacles in our dreams.

Clothing

One item often lost in dreams is clothing. We walk around in our dreamscapes only to discover with horror that we forgot to dress! Clothing represents our *persona,* the way we present ourselves to the world.[74] How we behave in society (and often even to ourselves) is not the same as who we really are inside. We show different aspects of the persona for different situations and people, and we need it in order to survive within our culture. From this point of view, when you dream of yourself naked, you are expressing a feeling of being vulnerable. At the university where I teach and where I have been collecting dreams for years, undergraduates in their first year tend to report the most suddenly naked dreams: they have not yet developed an academic persona.

You must reveal yourself with great courage every time you produce a work for the public. This feeling of exposure may also find its way into your dreams as the experience of being naked in public.

Parts of the Body

Some of our most horrifying dreams involve damaged or lost pieces of our bodies. It is worthwhile to consider what the body part does and what you may also be having difficulty doing at the time you have the dream. In a scene in one of his novels, John Nichols transformed a dream about trying to put strangers' body parts together into a scene in one of his novels. That, in itself, is a metaphor for what we do when we create. We try to put discrete, foreign, oddly fitting pieces together into a cohesive whole so that we can produce a work, or "body," of art.

This portion of a dream from Carlene combines the child theme from the last chapter with the themes of loss and body image. The dreamer is in danger of losing a metal stick figure. In the beginning of the dream, Carlene has a baby:

> She was in the image of a tiny blue metal stick figure. Kind of a defective kid, and I was disappointed at that and wondered about it at first. She couldn't move, so I had to look after her very carefully and carry her every-where. I was terrified of losing her. It seemed she could be very easily lost. I had seen her somewhere before she was born, in a window surrounded by bright light. She has [sic] a special spot on a wooden coffee table. I lived in a house with lots of healthy plants. I knew I wanted her to come more to life and finally she did. There were many people in the dream telling me how to take care of her and trying to help me, giving me advice. I was very happy in the dream.

Carlene's dream of the "defective" blue metal stick figure child says a lot about her relationship to her creativity. Before reading further, think a bit about what the dream might communicate about Carlene's creativity.

In the margin where she wrote down the dream, Carlene drew a picture of the child. It looks strikingly like a pen with two eyes. In fact, Carlene describes a shiny blue metal pen in her next dream. Carlene is a writer, and one wonders whether or not the pen she likes to use is made of blue metal and has its own place on the coffee table in her home. Did she first spy it in an illuminated shop window?

The dream also shows how, although she may now disparage it, nurturing, protecting, and admiring her creativity will bring her happiness she does not presently feel. She has support for her creativity from within—her "house" is full of life—and perhaps from without, as well.

If you came up with a similar picture, congratulations! You are well on your way to being able to apply these ideas to your own dreams.

Exercise: Fixing What's Broken

Glance over your dream journal, and note, below, each object that does not work properly, work at all, or perform the function it is meant to. Think about the object's purpose in the dream and describe that in detail. Next, consider: is there something you are trying to do in your creative life that you need the talent of this object in order to complete? Finally, take a look at what actually happens with the object in the dream.

In most dreams like these, the object never ends up working. In this exercise, try writing a new episode where you fix the object or find (or create!) another one that works as well or better. Visualize the scene. Imagine your delight when the object works, and envision the outcome. This exercise helps overcome creative blocks; what is "broken" is often what is blocking you! Doing this several times a week, or even daily, is quite effective.

OBJECT: _____

PURPOSE: _____

HOW/WHERE I NEED THIS IN MY CREATIVE LIFE:

_____

MY VISION OF A NEW OUTCOME:

_____

_____

Losing Our Minds and Losing Our Health

We meet all types of difficult situations in our dreams. We contract serious illness, lose our memories, become injured, or go insane. Dreams where these things happen to us and dreams of violence are described in chapter 8. Here, we explore dreams about *others* who are crazy and sick.

Eve tells of a particularly striking dream on this latter theme:

> I ask my ex-husband if he'd like to see the new house I bought, and he says sure. We turn at the end of the street where we were looking for something to eat. We get backed up in traffic. We go around the cars on the way to the house I bought for an investment. At this point almost everybody has been infected with the vampire virus and my ex-husband's eyes turn red and he develops fangs and his skin turns pale and he looks like he's going to attack me. He looks absolutely crazy. I'm not worried. I can take care of myself and he's not really harmful to me anymore.

What is happening here? Eve is driving and meets an obstacle in the road, but chooses to go around the block (so to speak). She has invited her ex to see her new house (a new house suggests Eve has changed a lot). As they are on the way to Eve's "new house," her ex transforms into a blood-sucking vampire.

From the outward path, others in dreams can represent outer reality (her ex is a vampire somehow). From the inward point of view (Eve's masculine qualities are like those of a vampire sucking her energy). And our outer experiences, including the people with whom we choose to interact, can mirror what is happening within us—the middle path.

Taking the perspective of the outward path, Eve might interpret the dream as a warning to watch out for vampire-like qualities in her ex. Does he "suck" her creativity dry? When she is with him, does she leave feeling less than she was before, depleted in some way, drained of energy? If so, the dream serves to remind her that she has changed; he is no longer able to harm her by depleting her creative energy.

From the inward path, Eve's dream suggests she has within her a threatening masculine energy that does what vampires do. It is difficult enough to create without having your life's blood flowing out of you. Like Rebecca, she may have had early experiences with a masculine person who did not support her emerging creativity, but drained it from her. As she grew up, she perhaps internalized that "vampire" so that it became active in her own mind (part III will elaborate on this theme).

Litton, an airbrush painter, also dreamed of what seemed to him to be a crazy stranger:

I am on a street at an intersection. I'm talking to a youngish man. He's heavyset. He's telling me about something that happened in the past, a shooting, how he shot at some people before. He's re-creating it for me. He punctuates his story by shooting near a crowd. One man says nothing and stands where he is, arms crossed. I admire his courage. He is not shooting close to me. The gun is oddly shaped, and when I think of it now, it looks like my portable touch-up paintbrush, which has a metal piece you can take off and protect the sable with. He has no feeling. He's just relating a story, like a psychopath. I am listening, genuinely trying to understand him. I am completely calm.

Prior to the dream, Litton had been in what he called "the insane period" in his work, portraying scenes of inner-city violence. It stunned him to imagine that his paintings might be affecting people in the same way as if he had shot them. "Then, again," he said, "isn't that why I paint to begin with? To wake people up?"

The lack of feeling in the dream troubled Litton. Remembering that lack of feeling in dreams can remind us we are unaware of our lack of feeling in life, the dream caused him to consider carefully his artistic motivations and emotional approach to his work. In contrast to the emotional flatness of the dream characters, Litton had become so carried away with the political implications of his art that he lost the sense of his purpose in creating—to arouse feelings of outrage, which might lead his audience to action.

Death

People who create frequently dream of death, the threat of death, and people they love, themselves, or even strangers dying. From the standpoint of the outward path, dream deaths may metaphorically represent the end or change of an actual living relationship with someone. When people are finally able to let go of an old and painful association, they often dream of the other person dying. They are able to move on; the other person is "dead" to them. What that person represented has become incorporated into the dreamer's own self. The other, although gone from the relationship, is still present within the dreamer's own soul.

From the point of view of the outward path, dreams of death can be remembrances of or preparation for an actual death of someone close. People who are faced with the terminal illness of a loved one or of themselves, or who are mourning someone who has passed away, dream more of death. Those dreams remain frequent for a time, until we have been able to move through the shock and most of the acute pain. But we continue to dream of people close to us who have died. Researchers have found that we dream of our parents, whether they are living or dead, with the same frequently throughout our lives.[75]

For those on the inward path, dreams of loss may reflect a part of ourselves passing away so that new growth can replace old patterns we no longer need. This is particularly true when we dream of our parents dying (as Rebecca recently did), long after they have really died, or when we have no reason to be concerned about their death in the present. As we mature, we cast aside the image of ourselves as our parents saw us, and become who we are, keeping some of their values, adapting others to suit our personalities, and discarding still others.

Throughout this process, our image of our parents also changes. They become real people, rather than all-powerful beings who hold the power of exaltation or humiliation, as they did when we were children. Their old images die in us, and may die in the mirror of our dreams. This process is necessary for us to come to our full potential as creative people. Otherwise, we may be creating to rebel, or creating to conform or to please our parents, rather than creating to fulfill and express ourselves, or to enrich our community.

People who create do have more dreams of death than do other people. No matter which path of interpretation we choose, each one involves the feelings that come from loss—sadness, abandonment, loneliness, relief, freedom, and, sometimes, accompanying guilt—when the dreaded thing has finally occurred. Most of these feelings are intense and uncomfortable.

If we did suffer an extreme loss in childhood, we were simply unable to deal with the feelings then. The overwhelming depth of feeling of a great loss is too threatening and dangerous for children who have not yet developed sufficient inner resources with which to cope. We hide the feelings to protect ourselves until years later, when we are strong enough to feel them.

When we go searching our depths for creative material, either intentionally or otherwise, we can come upon pockets of submerged memories and, sometimes, pain. We are unaware of them while we are awake, but they appear in our dreams and, when transformed, can inspire our most meaningful work.

░ ∼ ░ ∼ ░ ∼ ░ ∼ ░ ∼ ░ ∼ ░ ∼ ░ ∼ ░ ∼ ░

Exercise: Dream of Death

Dreams of death can alert you to what is passing away and what is coming to be within. How are you changing? What do you need to give up? To hold close? Humor? Cherish? If the person who is dying in the dream is yourself, in what ways are you already dead to feeling, to life? What could heal you?

Imagining that you are talking with your dream images is a powerful way of finding out what your death dreams might reveal. For this exercise, search through your dream journal or memory for a dream you had about death. What was happening in your life at that time?

If you are on the inward path, consider the character who died as a metaphor for some part of yourself, a quality you no longer need or have outgrown. What is the dying or dead character like? How would you describe him, her, or it to a friend who had never met the dead or dying character?

From the outward path, think back on all of your experiences with death. Does your dream replay them in some way? If you know someone who is dying or who has recently died, take comfort in knowing that your dream life is helping you cope with the loss. Healing takes time. Be gentle with yourself.

The middle path meets the other two paths. Could the part of yourself that is passing away be like someone who has actually died in your own life? Your dream characters can help you answer these questions.

Choose characters who are benign and unthreatening for this exercise. Relax and imagine yourself back on your chosen path. . .

After hours of wakeful hiding in a hollowed-out trunk, you realize it has gotten neither darker nor lighter. You emerge and make your way a little distance until you reach a square marble building, shining from the light of the stars and the moon. There are no windows and no doors. You run your hand across a strange symbol carved on one side. Suddenly, you find yourself inside. Soon, the character from your dream will appear. You are calm and know the other cannot harm you in any way, but is coming here to help you understand your dream. You hear a sound behind you, and turn to face your dream.

Start by introducing yourself to the dream character, thank him or her for coming, and explain that you would like help understanding the dream in which he or she appeared. Consider the questions posed previously, and ask those that seem most appropriate. After you have asked, pause and listen carefully in your imagination for the dream character's responses. If you get none at first, do not be discouraged. Some characters are shy, and this form of dialoguing with our inner figures takes practice. If at any time you become uncomfortable, you alone may leave the building by clapping your hands once. Stay until you feel satisfied, then clap and resume your journey through the woods.[76]

Leaving the marble building behind, you walk beyond a bend in the path and step over several fallen logs, mossy from the frequent rain. You bend to touch the silky moss and notice the fresh scent of the wood. Continuing on, you emerge suddenly on the edge of a crevice. Ahead is the sound of water. You step carefully around puddles and twigs, and are faced with an old, crumbling bridge of stone passing over a swift river. Embedded in it, worked loose by the rainfall, you spy a sparkling green gem. You pick it up. It is a shade you have never seen before: unusually clear, it holds the light. Looking ahead, you know you must cross, but the bridge looks precarious. Green stone in hand, you tentatively step between the rocks as the decaying wooden supports crack beneath your feet. Just a few more steps… The bridge trembles and shifts. The stones part. You fall! Cold. Something howls. Water in your lungs. You gasp, flailing and finally struggling onto the far shore. Your breath comes hard and your limbs hardly feel like your own. Lying alone and unable to move, you look up. The darkness is nearly complete now. A massive dark shape moves toward you. . .

≋ Chapter 7 ≋

The Theme of Inner Nature and Her Obstacles

OBSTACLES IN THE DREAMS of those who create are rarely people or things having to do with people. Rather, when creating, we are challenged in dreams by the natural world—waves, mountains, fires and floods, trees, deserts, stones in the road. These are difficult to interpret from the outward path; rarely are dreamers literally faced with boulders in the road, snakes, or rocky ravines. From the inward and middle path position, however, these dreams tell us a lot about the way we deal with difficulties in our creative work.

Bill, a thirty-nine-year-old writer who is having trouble with the latest novel he is writing, dreams he is driving down a street with a sharp ravine on one side:

> I approach an intersection and must drive around a big truck and backhoe that is chipping away at a boulder sticking partway into the street. There is another truck on the side street. I back away and I turn the wheel too sharply and my car starts going over the edge of the steep ravine...

As we saw in the last chapter, cars may represent movement in life, how we get from one place to another. A dream of driving is telling: how well are we piloting our own lives? Are we in control (driving)? Or is someone else? And if so, who? And to whom does our "car" belong—who is in control of our actions and decisions?

Bill is actively driving his own car, rather than being a passive passenger in someone else's. But there are natural dangers that keep him from getting to where he is going—a boulder in the road and a ravine. Bill begins driving just fine. He realizes there is a steep ravine next to him, but he is on course. The real danger strikes when, Bill tries to avoid the obstacle in his path.

What other options did the dream present? He could have driven around the boulder, as seemed to be expected of him. Or he could have taken a few deep breaths and slowly backed his car away. Perhaps he could have waited for the workers to finish demolishing what had "blocked" his path.

However, Bill told me that when he comes upon a problematic point in his fiction (what some writers call having written themselves into a corner), he becomes anxious and afraid that he has spoiled the entire work. Rather than writing around the problem for a while or continuing to "chip away" at it until a solution presents itself, Bill admitted that he tends to "back away" from it, trying to ignore it. Of course, the problem does not go away and his apprehension grows. Then, he tends to panic and "loses control," making moves within his fiction so drastic that the entire plot progression is threatened and thrown off course down the ravine. He literally goes "over the edge" in the dream.

A few nights later, Bill has another dream elaborating on this theme. He dreams he and a woman walk

> . . . out of the shadows of the green park and climb a narrow gravel path. Everything that looked green before is now brown. We look down off the edge of the path at a horde of dogs sitting below. "Look at all those dogs." We walk past and then by a small snake. She is in front and I tell her to watch out for the snake, but she is already past it. Then she walks by another snake which is on our left on a ledge (the ravine is on the right), and our path has suddenly become very narrow; the drop-off is sheer.
>
> She walks by the snake but I don't think I can get by it. It is a rattlesnake. She has come to a very steep area of rocks and I say it looks like we're stuck. She looks for a way down and says she found one, but I don't think I can get over to where she is. I'm afraid either the snake will bite me or I will fall off the ledge. "Do you think I should take a stick and try to knock this snake off?" I ask. She says she found the way; but I'm very scared, so scared I wake up.

Again, Bill comes to a natural obstacle on the path: a snake and a rocky ravine. Snakes are primitive symbols for the unconscious: they have the odd ability to sleep with their eyes open, always watchful. They also represent regeneration and, in the East, creative energy. Bill's companion does not fear the snake, but walks past it, taking the action necessary to find a way out of the dead end. The solution presents itself clearly in this dream in the form of the woman, a part of himself who knows the way and overcomes obstacles. Bill's greatest obstacle is his fear, which freezes him, and which he must face before he can move forward.

In his creative and personal lives, Bill is unable to conclude things. Endings frighten him with their finality. If he overcomes a problem in his writing, he must inevitably meet the end of his latest novel. If he works through a personal problem, he must move forward into a new, unknown life. This is the case with his dreams, as well. In a series of more than twenty dreams, none ends with resolution. However, Bill's dreams point the way to something beyond the obstacles; in each case, the road continues on. Bill's fear of nothing but oblivion being there when he resolves problems is an old fear, perhaps originating in childhood when loss and abandonment led to terror. Bill's challenge is not to avoid oblivion, but to find the courage to get there, and once there, to discover that all that awaits him is the endless, spiral path of his own creativity.

The dreams of those who create are filled with situations in which natural obstacles prevent us from getting somewhere we want to go. A dream of Mandy's, a twenty-nine-year-old painter, helped her realize the importance of her creative work. Mandy was at one of those places in life when it seemed easier to her to give up painting and join the corporate world. The decision left her feeling anxious, but she could not identify the source of her discomfort, feeling sure she had made the practical choice. On the eve of starting work in the human resources department of a computer software company, she dreamed:

> I am driving a sleek sports car and suddenly, very fast, I'm in deep water and water is flooding into my car. I try to get the window open, but the electrical system's damaged. I keep trying even though it seems hopeless, and I manage to open it. (The car is tilted downward and the window is upward.) I hear others telling me to get out now before the car sinks and I drown, but I want my things that would be impossible to replace—my driver's license with a strange landscape on it, sable brushes, and paper. At the last minute, I grab them and my purse and make it out safely.

Recall from chapter 2 that water is just about the only symbol experts agree on: it represents the life force, unconscious emotion. Mandy truly is in deep water, being flooded by strong feelings that overpower her in what she described as "a very ritzy car—I could buy that car in a year or two with this job." If she stays on that path, an expensive way of getting from one place to another, the dream warns she will drown. Best to get out now, and take with her what is most important: her identity as a landscape painter, the artist's path, tools, and blank pages.

"But what about my purse?" she wondered.

We discussed her conviction that she had to choose between earning a living and being an artist, and brainstormed ways she could do both. Mandy credits her dream for forcing her to recognize and honor what she knew inside all along: she cannot give up her art and still be herself. Mandy did not take the new job, eventually securing a position in an arts foundation to help make ends meet. She continues to paint, successfully exhibit her work, and helps others to do the same.

□ ≈ □ ≈ □ ≈ □ ≈ □ ≈ □ ≈ □ ≈ □ ≈ □ ≈ □

Exercise: Inner Nature in the Outer World

The landscapes of our dreams are some of the most artistic images we create each night. They may be vaguely familiar or a complete product of imagination. Often, as in dreams of natural obstacles, the arrangement of elements relates to the dream's meaning. Because the language of the dream is visual more than verbal, work-ing in pure images—by painting, drawing, making a mosaic, making a clay model, or even constructing a miniature scene—can help unlock the hidden meanings of a dream landscape. The next time you have a dream with a compelling setting, especially one that which stays with you for days, plan a project around it. In my dream workshops, participants have constructed their dream cottages, neighborhoods, rolling hills and valleys, and gardens out of wood, lichen, moss, and so on. Others have painted their dream landscapes onto dishes and had them fired at a pottery lounge. Famous painters have used their dream landscapes in their work. Why not you?

□ ≈ □ ≈ □ ≈ □ ≈ □ ≈ □ ≈ □ ≈ □ ≈ □ ≈ □

Air, Water, Earth, and Fire

Environmental obstacles can take an infinite number of forms. Each of the dreams in this chapter presents obstacles of either air, water, or earth, three of the four elements.[77] Everything in the natural world can be divided into one of them, and each is transformed into another through fire.

Air

Mythologically, air and breath are symbolically related, with air being a subtle material plane between Earth and the spiritual realms. In Christianity, for instance, air is related to the Holy Spirit. In some cultures, the wind is the messenger of God; in others, it represents the passions. Viewed from this perspective, dreams about hurricanes and tornadoes might indicate an overwhelming quickening of spiritual feeling or a building storm of creative energy within the dreamer.

Water

Water was discussed in a previous chapter as representing unconscious emotion. Water also corresponds to life, since all life needs water to survive. In ancient Roman temples, sick individuals would participate in rituals that would lead them to have a healing dream. Pilgrims, into the seventeenth century, sought healing dreams at thousands of sacred British wells, and early Christian churches were constructed over holy wells before the Roman church transformed them into baptismal fonts and brought them indoors.

Dreams of natural bodies of water connect us with our spirituality and with the vast unknown. As Stephen King said,

> I think that consciousness is like an ocean. Whether you're an inch below the surface or whether you're down a mile-and-a-half deep, it's all water. All H_2O. I think that our minds are the same nutrient bath all the way down to the bottom and different things live at different levels.[78]

Earth

Things grow out of the earth, and it provides nourishment for us, but the earth also takes us in the end. In most cultures, the ground is metaphorically associated with sensation, stability, and order. Psychologists speak of being "well-grounded" to describe a person who has his or her feet "on the ground"—a rational person. Tom Chetwynd, in his well-researched *A Dictionary of Symbols,* notes that, in ancient times, the earth was constantly threatened by the water of the sea, and that we have a similar fear of our rational and conscious mind being overwhelmed by the intuitive, feeling, unconscious self.[79] Mandy's dream of being in her car as it flooded with water and John Nichols's dream of flooding earth demonstrate that a balance needs to be found between feeling and thinking. We can do both and still be creative.

Fire

Fire is revered by many cultures as sacred and renewing. It destroys in order to purify and to aid in rebirth. Fire unites all separate elements and is required for their transformation. In chapter 2, we saw how fire can also represent passionate anger; some believe it symbol-izes sexual energy.

□ ≈ □ ≈ □

Misha's fire dream contains several themes we have discussed in this chapter and in the previous sections of the book. You might see elements in this compelling dream that seem familiar. Try to put them together and see what you come up with. Consider the images carefully before turning to the end of the chapter to learn more.

How much can you learn about Misha from this one dream without knowing anything else about her?

> I am in a meadow with trees all around. A wolf has a sheep in its mouth. I try to talk it out of eating the sheep. The wolf eyes me carefully. I appear calm, but am very frightened. This wolf could easily kill me. Yet, I continue to try to talk the wolf into letting the sheep go because it is innocent and powerless. I realize it is the wolf's nature to eat the sheep, but I'm hoping to save this one. The wolf listens, and the sheep drops away. Suddenly there is a loud noise and I see smoke. I tell the wolf we must run away; there is a fire. We run together, fast like the wind across the meadow, just ahead of the blaze. We come to a large group of elderly people. I know they will not all be able to move quickly enough to escape the flames. Some will die. The flames are close. I take the long way around to help people who are slower. On the dusty path I see a blue ceramic mask. It is very old. I pick it up, thinking I must have dropped it. It doesn't fit. I smash it to bits, feeling free.

Exercise: Overcoming Natural Obstacles

Taken from the perspective of the middle path, the dreams of loss described in chapter 6 whether they involve our possessions, people we love, strangers, the environment, or the self, are about our inner nature, which can get in the way as we travel on our creative path. Discerning the nature of the obstacle and keenly observing any clues to its dismantling that are presented in the dream will help us break free of patterns that can hinder our creative expression.

Look through your dreams for the natural obstacles that tend to get in your way. In the chart, jot down the obstacle, feelings you experienced, and the action you took in response to the obstacle within each dream. Do you see any patterns? You might want to go further by exploring similarities in what was occurring within the dreams when you came across the obstacles.

OBSTACLE	FEELINGS	ACTION TAKEN

Now, ponder how you respond to pitfalls in the practice of your work. How do you feel and what do you typically do when confronted with difficulty? Seek connections between those responses and your reactions to natural obstacles in your dreams.

Looking back at your dreams, do they present any alternative solutions that you have not yet tried? Think carefully about all of them, even if they seem unrealistic or impossible in waking life. For instance, if you dreamed you admired a bird flying beyond a washed-out bridge, you might consider the possibility of just flying away—taking a vacation by leaving the problem behind for a while. If you had dreamed of children joyfully leaping off the bridge into the river below, you might try holding your nose and diving into whatever feelings come up for you at this time. Find a way to try all possible dream solutions with your creative work. As always, treat your dream material and your own self with care. Never venture further into your dreams or the dark wood than you feel comfortable doing.

Now, look back at Misha's dream. At the time, she was a thirty-eight-year-old art therapy teacher living in a small Eastern town. She had the dream when she was trying to decide whether or not to leave behind the world of academia and become a practicing therapist. Both career options were appealing, and she was torn. Misha had struggled with her own feelings of sadness over a difficult childhood and early losses for much of her adult life. A few weeks after Misha had the dream, she read Clarissa Pinkola Estes's wonderful book *Women Who Run With the Wolves*.[80] Misha was inspired by the book and the dream. She learned from her dream that she was more frightened of the wolflike, animalistic, and sometimes violent urges she would witness as a clinician than she had realized. But she also learned she could "tame" them and felt she no longer fit her "blue" persona. After making her decision, her next dream seemed to confirm it:

> I am supposed to go from room to room, like on a golf course, tee to tee. The "rooms" are scattered outside. Some have doors; some, walls; and some, neither. I am naked. My task is to get from one point to another within the room before moving to the next. I'm alone. It's muddy. I put a foot on a ledge, pull up, place it back down, around. I get filthy. I feel I should be doing it better than I am. It seems endless. There are eight "rooms." I get to the end and it's been hard. The last one I almost didn't get. I go backward through them to the beginning and then realize, no! I don't need to do this again! I walk away.

Misha said the feeling of frustration in this dream helped her remember how frustrated she had been during each of the eight years it took her to come this far. She had never really felt adequate in academia, and she realized that much of what she was doing there seemed meaningless to her. The dream surprised her with its intensity of feeling. She realized she had not been paying attention to her feelings in her wish to make the most practical choice.

The dream did not make a decision for her; no dream should be allowed to do that. Rather, Misha's dream showed her places within herself she had been ignoring, and reminded her about what was most important to her.

Where We Have Been, Where We Are Going

In your journey into the woods, you learned about the creative process, what nourishes it and what depletes it, what might give you energy, and how to protect yourself from what might rob you of it. You saw how famous creative people have used their dreams, and perhaps been inspired to use your own. You also explored the three dream themes that distinguish the dreams of people who create from the dreams of others (loss, children, and natural obstacles), what they might mean, and how to unlock the gifts they offer to your creative life.

In part III, we venture into the heart of the dark wood, into our own psyches, to meet aspects of ourselves that can help or hinder our creative journey, dissolve blocks, and help us find unity and wholeness.

◻ ≈≈ ◻ ≈≈ ◻

The dark creature is just a little way off, now. You find that you are exhausted and can hardly move. There is no way back, anyway. The bridge is broken. You can only go forward. Seeking comfort, you flex your fingers. The jewel is gone. You must have let go of it in the river. The creature watches you, motionless beneath a lone tree in a small clearing. It is so dark you can see only its outline, the steam from its breath, and its glowing eyes. Your body jerks awake. You cannot tell how long you have been by the river, but with great effort, you slowly rise and walk toward the path. The creature seems to be gone, but the hair on the back of your neck is not so sure. As you reach the tree, the creature, remarkably agile for its size, leaps out and blocks your path. You are terrified, shaking uncontrollably, trying to stand there when everything within you is telling you to run. Running, you know, is futile. But having the courage to stand there and face this beast is the most difficult thing you have ever done. The creature makes a deep, low growl that rises into a howl. You close your eyes, certain this is where you will die. "What…do you want of…me?" you stammer. It bends its great head toward yours. You smell raw meat and blood on its breath. "Nothing, really," it growls. "What do you want of me?" In a quivering voice, you say, "My jewel, actually. I lost it in the water." The creature cocks its head, its fang-filled smile stretching its face. It nods, opens its enormous hand and drops the shining green gem into your palm. Like you, the jewel is a bit wet. You blow on it to dry it, and when you look up again, the creature has vanished…

Part III

Unlocking Our Creativity: The Dark Night and the Return

Midway on our life's journey, I found myself
In dark woods, the right road lost. To tell
About those woods is hard—so tangled and rough

And savage that thinking of it now, I feel
The old fear stirring: death is hardly more bitter.
And yet, to treat the good I found there as well

I'll tell what I saw, though how I came to enter
I cannot well say, being so full of sleep
Whatever moment it was I began to blunder

Off the true path. But when I came to stop
Below a hill that marked one end of the valley
That had pierced my heart with terror, I looked up

Toward the crest and saw its shoulders already
Mantled in rays of that bright planet that shows
The road to everyone, whatever our journey. . .

—Dante Alighieri, from *The Inferno*[81]

≋ Chapter 8 ≋

Those Who Block Us

When I paint I liberate monsters.
—*Pierre Alechinsky*

AT THE END OF THE LAST CHAPTER, you found yourself confronted by a vague and frightening beast, only to discover that by refusing to run away, you recovered a gift you thought was lost. In part III, you venture into the deepest heart of the dark forest, where you meet dangerous and helpful dream characters and come face to face with hidden parts of yourself, and, in the process, find more tools to unlock your creativity.

The path you are on is a lonely one, but nature offers its comforts. After your ordeals with the broken bridge, the water, and the creature, you pause to rest a while against an old fence in the shade of a tree.

Strange things happen in the forest when it transforms into a moonlit, starry place, with looming shadows and unfamiliar sounds. Odd people and animals can suddenly block your way, ask for something, or try to harm you. You have already met several others on your journey—the group in the meadow, the elusive child, dream figures in the marble room, and just now, a fearsome creature.

Travelers on the inward path understand that these frightening dream figures are parts of the self. We create them and take comfort in our implied power over them once we know who they are. Those on the outward path know there are similarities between dream figures and people in our real lives. The truth rests somewhere between these two positions, on the middle path. Not all of the beings who block our way are frightening, and as we will see in chapter 10, some can be quite helpful. But in this chapter we will meet dream characters who are simply annoying, and then progress to those we would rather not come across while lost in the deep, moonless forest. Our journey may produce unusually meaningful dreams. Continue to write them down. Danger is just ahead, but take heart: "the woods are lovely, dark, and deep. . ."

Dream Strategies for Overcoming Creative Threats

In the last chapter, Bill's boulders, ravines, and snakes kept him from going where he needed to go to complete his work. His obstacles were part of nature. They did not aggressively try to stop him; they just existed as barriers to this progress. In this chapter, we meet dream characters who intentionally interfere with us, actively attempting to sabotage our creativity.

Rather than dreaming of natural obstacles, Raine, a fiction writer, dreamed of humans who confronted her. The dream began with her sitting in a coffee shop, observing J. D. Salinger's characters, Franny and Zooey:

> Zooey was at his own table with a little boy with a flattop—his son? Did he have a wife? Well, anyway, my friend Helen diverted me from asking. Another friend of hers was there named Error. Error was embarrassing me. I said he made it so that I didn't like to go out with people I did not really know: "They scare me." Helen laughed at me when I said Error embarrassed me.

According to the dream, when Raine approaches her writing, her fear of making an error scares her from including new characters in her fiction.

The other characters in your dreams can lead you beyond your creative blocks even as they threaten you, and can alert you to paths that you would be better off avoiding. They do not speak to you in words you can understand, so rather than letting fear overtake you, be attentive to their metaphorical meaning. Sometimes these dream figures are easily recognized for what they are—ultimately impotent windbags, who can deter you from where you need to go only if you allow them.

Mallory, a midcareer advertising executive, had one such dream:

> I am walking and come to a street where there is a man with a hot-air leaf blower. It's like a propeller and doesn't affect the leaves much at all. There is a crowd waiting to

walk down the street, which, a long way off, is full of slick storefronts, very ritzy, where many successful people work. The man has cleared the street of people, though. One person walks through anyway, defying him. I follow, and others follow me. The man says it's our responsibility if we get killed (presumably by flying leaf debris, and he's serious) and tries to stop me by hurling all these insults. As I walk, branches, leaves, and twigs are blowing onto the street from machines on the side of the road. I keep walking, dodging the stuff. I reach the end of it. There is a curtain there. I walk through it and find myself amid the buildings I'd seen from far away.

Like Eve with her vampire ex-husband, but unlike Bill of the boulder and ravine, Mallory has learned that she must not allow her creative path to be blocked. During the year before she had this one, Mallory's dreams illustrated how she had become increasingly aware of the inner figures who tried to stop her from reaching her goals. They became more and more laughable, as with this man just blowing hot air. Mallory can now identify those at her workplace who would scatter leaves in her way, and rather than allowing them to distract or undermine her, she simply and confidently strides by them.

Threat and Coping: Key Questions to Ask of Your Dreams

Nevin, a young man of many talents, seems to be at an earlier stage of learning to overcome blocks when the way is in sight. An actor, photographer, and musician, he often finds himself creatively occupied in his dreams. He rarely expresses emotion in his frightening dream situations, suggesting that he may be out of touch with his fear in waking life (see chapter 2).

In one dream, a cult is trying to drug him with a potent drug that kills people by making them both passionate and sleepy. He escapes, but the cultists find him again when he stops to take a photograph "because the composition of the brick building and the staircases surrounding them is very beautiful." He jumps in a truck and escapes again, but discovers it needs new tires. When he stops to get them changed, Nevin decides to walk "around the street, looking for some textured painted wall to take a photograph of." Again, the cultists appear. This time, they catch Nevin. Nevin does not try to escape again. Instead, he remains cool and does not run, and the cultists are arrested.

Once Nevin stops running from his pursuers, he regains control of the situation and turns the tables on the blocking agent. Continuing to pursue his creative path without running away from the cultists seems to work. How does this strategy translate to Nevin's waking creativity?

To determine what your dream strategies may tell you about your creative process, you might ask these three key questions:

- What is the dream conflict or threat and when did it appear?

- What strategies did I use to cope with it?

- Were any of them effective? If not, what else might I have done?

Threat

The danger of being drugged asleep occurs now and then in dreams. It usually represents a present, real-life danger of becoming unaware, of "losing" consciousness. From the outward path perspective, someone in your life may be trying to keep you from being aware, awake, and truly alive. From the inward path point of view, such a dream situation reflects parts of yourself that would rather "put us to sleep" than…what? Determining when in the dream the threat first appeared can give you information about the purpose of the threat.

For Nevin, the cultists appeared whenever he began to practice his art. Could it be that in real life, Nevin is battling powerful others (represented by the cultists) who prevent him from expressing his creativity? Or does Nevin sabotage himself by losing his focus (being "drugged," running away) whenever he begins to create? Examining what Nevin does in response to the threat may provide a clue as to how he copes with creative blocks.

Strategies

Nevin copes, at first, by running away. Rather than confronting those who would try to drug him, Nevin tries to escape. That gets him nowhere, however, because as soon as he starts to create again, on come the cultists. He tries another strategy to remain cool.

Effectiveness

As long as Nevin stays self-contained and does not let his fear get the better of him, he prevails. This dream, and others in his series, suggest that this is true of his creative process, as well. Nevin may be afraid of expressing his creativity, perhaps because he was unsupported for doing so while growing up.

Through his dreams, Nevin could learn about his tendency to sabotage his creativity by either pulling himself back or "zoning out" just as inspiration overtakes him. He might find that some of the people in his life mirror this inner pattern. By seeking where the pattern began and observing it when it happens, Nevin can move beyond it, as Mallory did.

We can practice using these three questions with another of Nevin's dreams, which also lacks emotion. In this one, he is with another person, a stranger, on the way to see his grandparents. They are driving, actually flying just above the road. Just then, his companion suggests they go back and get Nevin's parents, and "I reluctantly agree":

> We turn around and go down a detour, an alleyway or a maze of highly colorful blocks; each block is a single color, smooth and shiny. People are walking around from block to block and our progress is very slow because of this. The "maze" gets narrower and narrower and more intricate as we go on. Finally, we decide to go carefully back the way we came.

Threat

Here, the trouble started for Nevin after he began to fly. We are exhilarated when we have the good fortune to fly in our dreams; rarely do we feel fearful. But his companion chooses that moment to interrupt Nevin's flight.

Strategy

Unfortunately, Nevin gives in to his companion and, like Bill, takes a detour from the path. Detours rarely lead us where we want to go; they distract us and take more time.

Effectiveness

This strategy does not move Nevin forward, but back to where he was before, where other people slow him down. What might Nevin have done differently in order to avoid getting "stuck" in a dead-end situation?

As suggested by this and other dreams, in his waking life, Nevin may be held back by another who brings him down to earth just as he begins to soar (outward path). He may also rein himself in, fearing his own freedom to create (inward path). Difficulty begins for him when he turns around and goes backward. His dreams hint that by remaining where he is, by being aware, facing the obstruction, and not running away, Nevin can get beyond what is stopping him. They also show him the folly of moving backward to old, familiar, ineffective ways of coping with difficulties.

You can overcome your blocks by paying attention to the themes in your dreams. The farther you progress on your journey to understanding yourself and your creative process, the stronger and more daunting those who confront you become. Before moving toward those more tenacious dream challengers, let's pause for an exercise.

◻〰◻〰◻〰◻〰◻〰◻〰◻〰◻〰◻〰◻

Exercise: Hiding from Ourselves

Relax, stretch yourself out like a cat, and let go of the cares that accompany you today. You will now find yourself again in the dark wood, having just encountered the creature. . .

You walk on in the only direction you can: forward. The bridge you had tried to cross was destroyed, and the river's waters are treacherous. The land here is wild and uninhabited. Although it seems no one has been here for many years, you can still make out the path ahead, overgrown and muddy in places. Low branches scratch your clothes, and their rich scent envelops you. You find your cloak has been ripped and is covered with drops of sap and dew. The forest is darker now, and you begin to stumble over the uneven earth. Strange sounds come from the deepest forest, and trembling from the cold and the unknown, you grasp your green gem. It glows a bit and gives you comfort. Tired, you edge off the path toward a little clearing. Something glimmers next to you. It is a stream, its waters cascading quietly down a small gathering of smooth stones. You move closer and see it sliding into a glass-like pool. Reminded of the meadow's pond, you look in but can see nothing but blackness. You blink, concentrating, but nothing is there.

Turning away and resting your back against a fallen tree, your thoughts pass over the many people you have known. You think about those you care for and those you do not, those you know well, and those who are strangers. Picking up your quill pen, you write the names of a few of those you think really well of, and then those qualities about them you most admire.

WORKSHEET A

ADMIRED PERSON (SAME SEX)	QUALITIES

All things exist in balance, and you also spend some time pondering those people to whom you have a strong negative reaction. For whatever reason, they just irritate you. These need not be people you know well. You write down their names and then those especially irritating qualities.

WORKSHEET B

IRRITATING PERSON (SAME SEX)	QUALITIES

Feeling weary, you wrap yourself beneath a tree in the underbrush for a rest. You smell the moist earth under the crisp leaves and needles. Hidden from danger, you daydream about the creature and other monsters you have known in your dream world and in your life, putting aside and saving what you have written for later...

Fearsome Others

You cannot harm me
You cannot harm one
Who has dreamed
Dreams like mine.

—*Ojibwa tribal song*

Consider the creature at the close of the last chapter. In the darkness, you could not get a good look at it. Its outline was vague. All you knew was that it was large in stature, made a growling noise, smelled like meat and blood, and blocked your way. The atmosphere of the wood enhanced the creature's frightening aura, and because the place looked like a setting for a horror film, the creature seemed dangerous. Really, it is just a carnivorous animal (as are many animals) that had obviously just eaten, and its growl is part of its everyday language. It is big, but again, its size is merely part of its nature.

Take the creature's point of view for a moment: here you are, bumbling about your favorite tree, when you smell something strange. This part of the wood suddenly reminds you of the time you saw your fellow creatures murdered by human hunters. You see a dim outline of someone crouched on the riverbank, perhaps with a gun! Perhaps ready to shoot! You hide behind the tree. The person slowly comes toward you. You have been found! You leap out, hoping for surprise, and let out your best, deep growl. The human does not run. You begin to get nervous, so you puff yourself up even larger, but the human stays calm and nonthreatening. Eventually, you realize this human is not about to harm you, and that you have in fact inadvertently swiped a lovely sparkling thing that the human would like back...

We fear the unknown because what is unfamiliar may hurt us. The patterns in our dreams portray how and by whom we expect to be hurt. They also show us what we often do to avoid the fearful situation. Running away never works, because what we fear and run away from keeps returning to block our creative expression. In order to break through, you need to confront and trace the outlines of what you fear until they become the contours of your own face.

The hardest thing to do in a dream can be to stop running long enough to confront the thing that is chasing you, and harder still is to ask what it wants. When you do, you find a fearful part of yourself trying to transform into something that can be helpful. I often advise my clients to ask their dream pursuers for a gift. The gift represents the dreamer's new self-insight.

We will now meet the creatures who aggressively block our paths. What can they can tell us about our creative blocks?

The Dark Shadow

As we become acquainted with parts of ourselves that prevent us from fully expressing our creativity, new characters confront us in our dreams. How frightening they are and how familiar they seem depends upon the depth of our acquaintance with ourselves. Dreaming of an alien robot chasing you might indicate that the quality the creature represents is far away from consciousness (for example, you do not realize how overintellectualized and mechanical your approach to life has become). A menacing character that looks like a cross between your partner and the Tin Man from *The Wizard of Oz* might mean that you are close to becoming aware of the mechanical quality of your life.

Jung called those parts of ourselves of which we are not aware the *shadow*.[82] The shadow contains not only qualities we consider negative and would rather not acknowledge, but also positive qualities that challenge our self-image. Look back at what you wrote on Worksheet A on page 142. According to this point of view, qualities you admire in others are also shadow qualities of your own that you need to become aware of and honor in order to express yourself more fully.

Mandy, whose natural obstacle dream in the last chapter (of nearly drowning in the sleek car) helped her realize how important her art was to her, had this striking dream once she began to pursue her new life:

> I am with a dark woman. She lives in a house near the sea. I've come to tell her my admiration for her, which is tremendous. She has it all together: some kind of artist, she's risked everything for her life, and is very interested in what I think. Just then a man drives by, he's an actor from some TV show, but she says, "Uh-oh. I knew this would happen." It is "Bob," (a stranger) who I think has come to punch me in the face. I get my keys ready to jab him if he tries. He comes in and there are suddenly several people there, all checking out my suitability for their group, being sociable. The man comes in, but he can't stop me, he can only intimidate me.

Mandy's positive shadow qualities are reflected in the dark woman. (We will explore the negative "Bob" type of character in the next chapter, and more positive dream figures in chapter 10.)

According to this perspective, not only positive characteristics, but also those qualities that irritate you when you meet them in other people are also reflections of yourself. "Negative" shadow qualities are much less enjoyable to see than are the "admirable" ones! But those qualities we think of as unbecoming or negative also need to be recognized and expressed. They become even more obvious and irritating in others just before we become aware of them in ourselves. Even very negative qualities can be positive attributes in specific situations! No quality is, in and of itself, negative or positive.

The process of becoming more deeply familiar with yourself is even more important for those who create, because the shadow is the seat of creativity: it contains your potential. Shadow qualities that make themselves known to you through other people can be exactly those qualities you need to develop (in, perhaps, less extreme form!) in order to be more creative.

You might want to summarize those qualities you mentioned in Worksheets A and B on page 142 here, especially noting those that occurred more than once:

_____

_____

_____

_____

We can be unaware of both negative and positive qualities within us. Do you see any trace of these characteristics in yourself? These might be aspects of yourself you need to develop right now, in order to express yourself more fully and creatively. Try not to judge them (or yourself!).

For example, if you wrote "loud" or "obnoxious," you may be unaware of (and consciously need to express) your capacity to be loud and obnoxious (or perhaps just assertive!). In order to become conscious of those qualities, you might try making up a plan for yourself where for ten minutes you consciously attempt to be "loud and obnoxious" in a positive, less extreme way. To do this, you will need to consider the positive uses of loudness and obnoxiousness: for instance, loud and obnoxious people do tend to get heard and are not easily pushed around. As part of your plan, you could calmly give your opinion in a group where you would normally be silent. Or you could find a place to be alone or with a few friends, and play at being rambunctious. Your goal is to express, in a constructive way, those qualities of which you were consciously unaware until now.

One of the shadow qualities with which many of the dreamers in this book struggle (including Diana, below) is that of being critical of themselves and their creative work. When she performed this exercise, Diana discovered that "critical" frequently appeared on her list of irritating characteristics. Diana had high expectations of herself and others that they (and she) could never possibly meet. Having been raised in a home of perfectionists, she felt her expectations were reasonable. In fact, they set her up for failure.

After discovering "critical" on her list, she decided to "pretend" she was a critical person, using one of her dream images as a guide. One of her friends acted the part of Diana, while she played the critical one from her dream. She was surprised to find that the role came naturally to her, and she began to question how critical she might really be. During this exercise, Diana learned new phrases from her friend to use in response to criticism, such as, "I'm doing the best I can," "Thank you for your honesty; I'm sure you're only trying to be of help," and "You have no right to judge me." Diana discovered she could be critical of the criticizer: "If you like, I can list all of your faults, too!" The most important thing Diana found, though, was that the critical one was a liar, willing to say anything about her in order to reach its goal—her own immobilization. She felt its fear when her friend did not respond to criticism. Diana even felt some compassion for that frightened part of herself bent on paralyzing her creativity.

But shadow qualities are supposed to help us, once we become more aware of them. How could Diana, by becoming more critical, unlock her creativity? The exercise showed her that she really was critical of herself and others and needed to learn how to become more appropriately critical: she needed to consider critically what stood in the way of her being creative (her too-high expectations). Diana needed to learn to critique her work from a positive standpoint, because good critics also applaud those they evaluate.

Doing something playful to express shadow qualities can lend some humor to an otherwise uncomfortable realization. It can also afford you some perspective on your "faults." Every quality can be useful and positive in some circumstance. Once you have identified the positive possibilities of the shadow, play them out and see whether you don't feel more creative energy afterward. Try to do the exercise in this chapter once every few months. The content of the shadow changes as we become more or less aware of various aspects of our personalities.

As I was beginning to write this chapter, I had the following dream:

> I am taking photographs of the ocean. Later, I get them back. I look at the pictures and see the shadow of a large bear. Good! I think. Now everyone will believe me: there really was a bear! The bear is on its hind legs, swiping at someone in one picture, and walking along in two others. A friend points to its nose.

When I woke, puzzled from this dream, I remembered the announcer's voice for The Shadow, a radio-character-turned-movie-hero: "The Shadow knows!" My dream pun (nose/knows) reinforced for me how shadow characters can tell us a great deal about ourselves and our creative process.

All of the dreamers we have met so far in this book are dreaming of their own shadows. Some of their dream characters do exist in the real world, and the dreamers' interactions with them mirror what happens when they meet while awake (an outward path perspective). But, as we have seen, these dream characters also represent aspects of the dreamer's own self, the province of the inward path. Discovering the meeting place between inner dream characters and outer people in the world, we can walk the middle path. It is challenging to look carefully at what you wrote in the worksheets on page 142. But the more you look, the more you will really see. Not all of it will be pleasant, but it is all useful, as we will learn in the second exercise, near the end of this chapter.

The First Stages of Knowing Our Dream Selves

The shadow emerges in dreams in different ways. We go through several stages in our journey to get to know those inner figures who block us. These stages find their metaphorical way into our dreams. As we begin to become aware of and integrate an emerging shadow quality into our self-image, we may dream of threatening animals. As we become more aware of this emerging quality, the shadow often manifests itself as a human, a threatening stranger. (In the next chapter, we explore further stages of shadow awareness in our dreams.)

Stage One: Threatening Animals

What is most unfamiliar within us can first emerge in our dreams as an animal, or even an alien or some other nonhuman creature. Its very form seems to say, "This Thing is different from me! This cannot be me—it isn't even human!"

In this first stage of shadow awareness, we are almost completely unaware that we, ourselves, are blocking ourselves. As do many of the dreamers in this book, we might attribute our inability to create to all kinds of outside factors: the weather, lack of support from others, financial constraints, or the atmosphere of our homes. Each of these can certainly impinge upon our ideal creative situation. However, few well-known creative people had ideal conditions for creativity before becoming successful. Most worked hard, catching their ideas drifting through their heads while doing the dishes with babies crying in the background; or they worked at their beloved crafts in the middle of the night while spending days at a job that did not fulfill them. Many suffered through adverse sociocultural conditions and environmental stress, making it more difficult to retain their energy to create. Whatever time and energy you can find to devote to your creative activities, do it, remembering that others have struggled, persevered, and become successful. And the next time you give yourself a reason for not expressing yourself as creatively as you would like to, thoroughly question yourself. Then, look closely at your dreams.

As you do, you may find what Pamela, a budding fashion designer attending a competitive design school, did. She entered my office, dressed in white, as she often was—this time in a fluffy sweater—and related her dream:

> I was petting a white kitten. It was very cute and sweet and nice. It got scared if I moved too quickly and unexpectedly. Then it would become a poisonous snake and bite me. I had to be very careful and go very slowly.

Pamela's kitten looked very much like her. Not only does Pamela like to dress in white, but she also speaks softly and keeps her fingernails long, pointed, and painted red. Cats represent the feminine in most cultures,[83] so I was curious about how Pamela's feminine qualities were faring.

After telling me the dream, Pamela said, "I hate cats. I had a cat once who was afraid of everything. That's probably why I had the dream." Pamela describes herself as "fearless—I'll take anybody on!" Her self-image is based on her perseverance and on her unwillingness to be victimized as she aggressively and competitively pursues her career. Sometimes this gets her into trouble, as she knows how to insult people, "to really hit them where they live." At the time she had the dream, she believed other people were deliberately provoking her. She is a strong woman, having returned to school in midlife, and her classmates tell her that when she is not cutting them down, she can be fun to be around.

In working with her dream, Pamela first answered the three key questions on page 137. She was threatened by the cat, who initially seemed innocuous but became dangerous when frightened. In order to cope with the danger, Pamela moved slowly. The dream did not continue long enough for her to discover whether or not this strategy worked. After discussing her responses to this frightening dream, Pamela acknowledged that although she keeps her claws pointed, she has a vulnerable side that reacts strongly and defensively to sudden changes.

We decided to work with the outward perspective first, formulating a plan for Pamela to use in dealing with her classmates, who she believed provoked her into "biting" them. Pamela agreed to monitor her outbursts at her classmates for one week. She was sure she would learn that they were picking on her. When she returned to my office, she was unusually pensive. She had discovered that her angry put-downs were not provoked: on the contrary, Pamela responded that way whenever others *praised* her.

"It's been happening quite a bit, lately, the compliments. There's such pressure. I'm so nervous. I'm actually beginning to believe that I'm going to make it. It's terrifying, really, and it's happening so fast."

At the end of this session, Pamela stretched, rose, and vowed to trim her nails a bit and to think before biting. Over the next few weeks, Pamela surprised everyone, including herself, by holding her tongue. She reported feeling anxious during this time, but was not sure why.

Soon, she felt unable to continue her work, had no ideas, and no motivation to keep trying. She was restless and worried. She wondered whether she was simply the kind of person who needed to take jabs at other people in order to pull herself up, and that question in her mind left her feeling even worse.

We had come to the crossing of the paths, and one day Pamela tentatively moved toward the inward one: "I feel like I'm attacking myself." Remembering that our outer world often reflects what is happening within us, Pamela began to explore the ways in which she (like Nevin) pulled herself down, insulting herself just when she began to feel that success was possible.

In chapter 3, we saw how famous creative people often come from homes in which they were not seen or valued for who they were. It becomes quite difficult for them, as adults, to encourage themselves, and far safer to attack themselves before the others they are sure will attack them, do so. That was Pamela's situation. She had always wanted to design clothes and was continually ridiculed for it while she was growing up. In order to ease the pain she was getting from others who professed to care about her, Pamela developed a way of protecting herself: she bit first. If someone complimented her, she not only negated the comment by ignoring it, but she actually punished the person.

Pamela did not start this behavior because she was cruel. Instead, it was the only way she could initially protect herself from the crushing blow of being admired and then "stabbed in the back," as she put it, "when they took the compliment away with some snide comment." She began to see that her family and friends had been insecure and perhaps even jealous of her talents, and that their feelings and inappropriate behavior had little to do with her.

Pamela's challenging task would be to change a pattern that originated at a time when it was needed. Now, instead of being helpful, that pattern had become a harmful habit. Pamela practiced observing her feelings when praised, and when she felt a bit of fear, she immediately imagined herself in the dream. She envisioned petting and soothing her dream cat, telling it these people would not harm it. If they did, Pamela promised the creature she would protect it.

Pamela eventually stopped biting, hissing, and growling at others who praised her. Her threatening (and threatened) animal dream helped Pamela learn about a frightened part of herself that was uncomfortable to see, but valuable to meet and pay attention to.

Stage Two: Dangerous Strangers

The next stage of familiarity with the shadow that is represented in our dreams happens when we are beginning to know our creative saboteurs. It is that of the dangerous stranger. Sometimes, we fear shadow figures for no apparent reason; other times, they can be violent, and our dreams become nightmares. Their frightful nature invites us to look more closely at the degree to which we are aware of our fear in waking life, and in what ways it may be holding us back. For example, Anne Rice tells of a dream she had as a child of a shadow figure—an elderly woman made of marble whose appearance terrified her. Stones and marble have several meanings in different cultures. In the United States, "she is made of stone" is a metaphorical way to describe an emotionless person. Marble stones also mark Western graves, and are thus associated with death.[84] The image of the stone woman remained with the author, and eventually appeared in the vampire series as a powerfully horrifying image that we intuitively understand. Emotionless beings can be dangerous and scary.

Gillian, a university professor, dreamed the following, transparent shadow dream:

> A girl, eighteen or twenty years old, with stiff, white makeup and black lips and hair (looks like one of my creative students who constantly challenges me), storms into my office, expecting maltreatment. I realize she wants my attention. She is furious and feels ignored and mistreated.

From the outward path, we could explain this dream by saying that it expresses what is really occurring between Gillian and the student. When we ask why she had this particular dream at this particular time, we move inward and find that, having been caught up in her intellectual, academic mode for nearly a year, Gillian has found little time to nourish her creative work (sculpting). Her creativity is in danger of dying.

In each of these "fearful other" dreams, treasure can be found. But as in all good fairy tales and adventure stories, the hero does not find the gold without risk, danger, suffering, and the willingness to continue when all hope is lost.

Keeping in mind that threatening strangers often mirror shadow qualities with which we have yet to be acquainted, read Devon's dream and try to discover what the dreamer is beginning to acknowledge about herself:

> I was staying with my mother. Some girl with dark hair was there, too. At first, she was sort of a friend of mine. Then I got suspicious of her for some reason and kept my distance. I didn't like to get too close. I was trying to make a cake with a huge two-dimensional egg beater made out of roses. I was feeling I had no space. This woman had taken over the place. I was mad at her. I went out back (now it was my childhood backyard) and yelled at her. She was cold. She came in and wanted to watch *Dracula*. My mother was on her side and really liked and enjoyed her. Finally, I was with my mother and I said, "You wish she were your daughter instead of me, don't you?" and she answered, "Yes, I do," smiling and pleased with the thought. She went on and on about it. I got mad and yelled and said I couldn't believe she felt that way, that I would never trust her again. Never. That I was insulted by all the times she said we were friends. Incredible hurt. I wanted the girl to leave now. She was like a neighbor from childhood—very intellectual, dull, snobby, and superior.

The first thing to notice about the dream is its feeling tone. We can initially surmise that Devon is angrier than she is aware of being, and that she may need to feel her anger in order to release it. We begin to work with this dream by answering the questions from page 137: What is the threat that makes Devon so angry? When did it occur? What does the dreamer do to cope with the threat? Does it work? If not, what else might the dreamer have done?

Here are Devon's responses, recorded on a worksheet you will use for your own dreams later in this chapter:

KEY QUESTION WORKSHEET

THREAT	Girl (intellectual, snobby, dull, superior) takes over
WHAT I DID	Distanced myself, tried to keep creating
DID IT WORK?	No, it made the situation worse and Mom loved her

In this dream, Devon is threatened by a strange girl who, when Devon is trying to create something, intrudes on her, "takes over," and even steals her mother's love. Although Devon was initially friends with this girl, she was suspicious and "didn't want to get too close." As with so many of us, Devon was made uncomfortable by the qualities this girl represented within her and, rather than getting near them to look at them more closely, Devon avoided the girl who embodied them in the dream. The dream went downhill from there.

Consider what Devon wrote in the worksheet. If her dream mirrors her waking life, what happens to her when she begins to work creatively? Is she avoiding some "negative personality" characteristics of her own, and if so, which ones?

Looking at this dream (echoed in many others from this period) from the perspective of the inward path, we can guess that Devon's mother's attitude toward Devon's creativity still lives within. When Devon begins to create, the intellectual side of herself (which she sees as dull, snobby, and superior) takes over, and makes it difficult to open up to new ideas and creative play. Devon is also troubled by what she sees as her mother's preferring her "shadow sister" to her more creative self. From the outward path view, the dream shows Devon feels angry and hurt by her mother's rejection of her, and is probably not aware of just how much she is affected by her mother's behavior.

Integrating these interpretations with facts about Devon's life leads us to the middle path. Devon had attended an Ivy League school and majored in mathematics, but transferred elsewhere in her junior year to learn to become a graphic artist. She was now a successful freelancer, but her friends resented what they interpreted as pretentiousness when they saw her striking out confidently on her own. Also, Devon felt guilty for having rejected her mother's alma mater. Her mother had never openly told Devon of her disappointment, but Devon sensed it. Until she had this dream, Devon denied feeling angry or upset at her mother for being unwilling or unable to accept Devon's choice or to be enthusiastic about Devon's artistic talent. In time, Devon was able to let go of the hope that her mother would choose to support her career, but she did calmly discuss her hurt feelings and anger. That conversation eased some of the tension between mother and daughter and made it easier for Devon to value her creativity.

◻ ∼ ◻ ∼ ◻ ∼ ◻ ∼ ◻ ∼ ◻ ∼ ◻ ∼ ◻ ∼ ◻ ∼ ◻

Exercise: Confronting Dream Threats

Read your last several dreams and choose one in which there is a shadow figure. Fill in the worksheet, using Devon's as a guide. Make sure you describe the qualities of your confrontational dream character as honestly as possible:

KEY QUESTION WORKSHEET

THREAT	
WHAT I DID	
DID IT WORK?	

Consider how the strategy you used to cope with a dream threat relates to the way you handle threats to your creativity when awake. Has the strategy you have been using worked? Might you try another? If you have difficulty coming up with alternative strategies, place yourself back in the dream and imagine what you might have done differently within the context of the dream. Translate the new strategy to your waking life: make a plan for implementing it the next time you feel your creativity threatened or blocked.

□≈□≈□

Once you identify the threat in your shadow dreams, what you did to cope with it, and whether or not that strategy worked, you get a glimpse of how unknown or barely acknowledged inner obstacles block you and how you can get beyond them. But getting to know your negative shadow qualities by searching through your dreams is unpleasant at best and frightening at worst. Shadow dreams typically evoke strong feelings, or else you feel no emotions at all, even in situations that would normally terrify you, reminding you that these are dreams to examine further. Seeing yourself as you are, no matter how ugly the reflection, brings with it humility, honest self-knowledge, and the opportunity to transform these frightening inner qualities into positive, integrated parts of yourself.

As you become more familiar with shadow qualities in the first two dream stages, they begin to take the form of people you know and, at last, of yourself. In the next chapter, we explore these last two stages of familiarity.

□≈□≈□≈□≈□≈□≈□≈□≈□≈□

Safe under the shelter of the trees, you crawl to the edge of the pool, trying to peek out of the corner of one eye so that, if what you see there is too horrifying, you can quickly look away. An ugly creature whose face is covered with warts and small craters stares back at you. You instinctively pull back. Taking a deep breath and reassuring yourself that this is only a reflection, you look more closely. There is something in the creature's face that looks familiar—there, around the eyes. The qualities you wrote about earlier come to mind. Feeling humbled, you flinch a bit, but continue to look at the mirrorlike pool...After a time, ripples cross the surface. Feathers beat overhead, and a square of parchment paper drops to your lap. Stunned, you unfold it and read a passage you recognize as being from Rainer Maria Rilke:

> Perhaps all the dragons of our lives are princesses who are only waiting to see us once beautiful and brave. Perhaps everything terrible is in its deepest being some-thing helpless that wants help from us.[85]

You move on through the trees. The path has become quite overgrown and hard to negotiate in the lingering dusk. You must leap over fallen trunks while avoiding the deep crevices on either side of the path. Once, you nearly slip, and are shaken by the sound of stones falling endlessly down the ledge a mere foot away. There is nothing picturesque about this place. It is barren in its overgrowth. Feeling alone and in peril, you can count on no one else for help. You become confused and cannot remember why you set out upon this path. Turning around, you freeze. Was that a footstep you heard? You continue on ahead...

You have heard footsteps behind you for some time now. Too afraid to stop, you keep walking down the narrowing path. You can almost feel breath on the back of your neck when you reach a high stone wall. There is nowhere to go.

The footsteps come faster, closer. You claw at the wall, terrified. Something comes off in your hands. A door in the wall opens, blocked by a tall, expres-sionless person. "Halt," a voice rumbles. "You may not pass." Looking beyond you, the gatekeeper goes pale and pulls you into a tiny closed chamber within the wall. There is a door on the other side, but it is locked fast. An emblem of a person with two faces, one looking outward and one inward, is carved over the door.

"You are being pursued by an evil one," says the gatekeeper. "You have trespassed here. You cannot continue on without the great key that will turn the lock."

Close to despair, you beg the stranger to let you pass.

"Without the key, you must leave the way you came and deal with your pursuer as best you can. I must tell you that no one has survived to escape that way."

Panicked, you persuade the gatekeeper to allow you a few moments alone. Trying to quiet your heart and gather your thoughts, you sit on the dank, cold stone floor...

Chapter 9

Blocking Ourselves

What doesn't kill me makes me stronger.
—*Friedrich Nietzche*

AT THIS POINT IN YOUR JOURNEY, you are no longer dreaming of strangers and animals who mirror unknown parts of yourself. Now your dreams come closer to "home," filled with people you know, and even yourself, acting in unusual and exaggerated ways. These dreams fill you with emotion. Anger, fear, guilt, or sadness explode within them, you may wake shocked and exhausted.

Unless you prepare yourself for the task of unmasking your shadow, you can become overwhelmed and full of despair when your awareness of yourself grows to accommodate your threatening aspects. Just as you previously thought you had none of these uncomfortable qualities, you may now believe this is all you are.

It will help to remember that neither perspective is true. We all have the capacity to express any characteristic given the proper circumstances. Having this capacity does not mean we will actually do these things, which is what separates us from those who commit evil acts. If we dream of ourselves or those we love saying or doing terrible things, it usually means only that something within needs to be addressed; the neglected aspect is portrayed so dramatically in our dreams to get our attention. If we dream of hurting another person who is dear to us, we probably need to explore and feel our anger for that person constructively and safely; we do not need to hurt him or her as we did in our dream.

We all have unpleasant impulses that, for the most part, we do not act upon. But to place ourselves above others who do what we do not approve of is part of denying the shadow within. At certain points in the journey, before we can come to know ourselves and to find and release the energy required to overcome creative blocks, we may become sensitive to certain kinds of people. Suddenly, the world may seem filled with them—people who take up too much space, people who hurt other people, people who restrict others' freedom, critical people, suffocating people. We see them everywhere. We begin to stereotype. The world takes on a hopeless, dark cast. We alone, or we and our friends, are above this sort of behavior. It is the cruel world out there that is the problem. *If only it weren't for them...*, we think. In our first efforts to see the difficult truth of ourselves, the *collective Shadow* is often revealed to us.

The collective Shadow (capitalized to different it from personal, individual shadow characteristics) contains all of those qualities in humans that we, as a species, would prefer not to acknowledge: the feelings, impulses, and behaviors that are unacceptable, no matter where we live. Coming face to face with the Shadow can be paralyzing. Depending upon how deeply we glimpse it, it leaves in its wake hopelessness and horror. Those who have had the misfortune to be marred by human violence have been touched by the Shadow. It is what inspires us to ask questions like, "How can people do that to one another?" "How will the world survive?" "What is the point of living if all there is under the surface of life is this horrible truth?" Some things we humans have done and can do are evil acts, but one sign of being immersed in the Shadow is a feeling that evil is pervasive. We lose sight of the other side. We are out of balance. Sometimes, this confrontation happens just before we recognize the need to find out about something threatening within. It often coincides with dreams of familiar people, in which either they or we are behaving in a way we can only regard with horror.

The three key questions we used in the last chapter often do not go deeply enough for dreams in these two stages. In them, your dreams are particularly upsetting and often even horrifying, for you have traveled beyond the personal shadow into the realm of the Shadow.

Stage Three: Our Dark Side in People We Know

There is no birth of consciousness without pain.

—Carl Jung

Michael, an artist, struggled with shadow in his dreams. He had rejected his father, refusing to see him after the older man confessed that, although he wished he could, his values did not allow him to support Michael's bohemian lifestyle. Michael's father repeatedly tried to find a way to meet Michael halfway, but Michael was stubborn, even though he knew that this separation was hurtful to both him and his father. Michael had a vision of the way he thought his father should be, and when his father could not conform to it, Michael broke with him. Oddly enough, Michael could only see the rigidity of his father's view and was unaware of his own.

Michael found himself in the province of the Shadow when his father unexpectedly died soon afterward. Michael could no longer work, fearing his art had lost its value for him. Suddenly, all around him, he saw people who did not care for one another. He commented on how "no one cares about anyone else anymore; they just want to take what they can get," and "no one wants to give." His chief topic of conversation became the breakdown of the family. Older people living alone, without families, particularly touched him.

Even so, Michael was unable to relate his new perspective to his rejection of his father. As long as he focused on what was going on out there in the world, he could avoid turning inward. After weeks of increasing despair, Michael had a series of short dreams, culminating in this one:

> We are outside in a park, perhaps in the cemetery. My father crawls through the dirt toward me. I begin to kick him. He is begging me to stop. I kick and kick. He is covered with dirt. It gets in his eyes and mouth. I do not stop. I keep kicking. Finally, my father stops moving.

Michael awoke from this dream horrified at his own behavior. Tears were flowing down his cheeks.

When I next saw him, Michael's bearing had changed. Instead of the self-righteous anger I had seen the week before, Michael looked deflated, as if he had himself been kicked. He realized that his anger at his father had been turned on the whole world, and that those people at whom he had been angry were no worse than he was. Michael had "kicked" his father when the older man had tried to be honest, and had spurned his attempts at reconciliation. Now it was too late. He felt responsible for contributing to the stress that led to his father's heart attack: "I broke his heart."

After working with his dreams and expressing his long-buried fear, hurt, and anger, Michael began to have compassion for the failings of other people, because he could see his own. He could see beyond the Shadow. But he turned his hostility on himself, ignoring his positive qualities and the love he really felt for his father. Michael turned himself into a monster in his own eyes. He was only able to see the negative shadow, and he still could not work.

This is the point at which the journey becomes particularly perilous. Hopelessness and despair possess us and we cannot find the door that will lead us away from this barren, dry, and dusty-feeling place. Like Michael, we are painfully aware of our shortcomings and failures, of the ways in which we have hurt others. We feel (and are) alone with ourselves. Others do not understand, and do not seem to want to hear the truth of what we are feeling, even if we could tell them about the depth of it. This stage can result in depression, which is associated with creativity in prominent people (see chapter 3). People who are sensitive and intuitive are often more aware of the injustices and suffering in the world, and are perhaps more prone to these dark shadow periods as a result.

Monica, a successful writer, had these dreams after being confronted with the shadow by her ex-husband of several years, who had become a close friend. For several weeks, she had been unable to write. After a period of time in which Monica became particularly irritated by others whom she described in just the same way her ex-husband had described her, she was devastated to realize these adjectives described herself as well. No longer sure of who she was, Monica lost sight of all of her positive characteristics and was swallowed by the negative side of the shadow (and by the collective Shadow, as we shall see).

When reading her first two dreams, see whether you can identify the shadow qualities with which Monica was confronted:

DREAM ONE: I was in a foreign country. It was unbearably hot. My friend, Jane, had been caught breaking some obscure rule she didn't know about, that didn't make any sense. She was to be killed. A huge, muscled, and strong man was filling a hypodermic with poison or an air bubble or something. She was really naive and didn't realize they were going to kill her. She trusted them. I hated her for that, for her quivering weakness. Time was running out. I was really angry and appalled and planned to do something to save her, but I didn't know what.

DREAM TWO: I was walking down a long, cobbled path with Peter (my ex-husband). I realized we were in hell. Peter was determined to do something about it. We were going to find my friend, Christine. She was trapped there in some kind of lab for an experiment. We wanted to get her out. As we walked down the incline, I began to tell Peter to watch out for the despair that comes from this place. To expect it. We got to where Christine was. She was guarded by some men, mad scientist types, not allowed to leave, but not locked in. I told her I had a plan. I was going to use thick makeup to make us look like other people. We'd break the glass, jump through, and run. I thought it would work. She was wearing fine lace, a skirt and blouse, very thin and fragile. We were sly and the guards didn't suspect us. It was their job to keep Christine there.

These dreams give us a picture of two parts of Monica's psyche: one who is naive and fragile and beginning to be recognized (the shadow), and another who is competent and knows exactly what the danger is (Monica's conscious personality, who she thinks she is).

Monica prided herself on being self-sufficient and independent. She described herself as an honest and kind person. Having had a difficult childhood, she also felt deprived of affection and respect. Monica had a pattern of becoming involved with others who were threatened by her talent and would, out of insecurity, try to sabotage her. Although friends would warn her about these individuals, she had a blind spot when it came to trust. After her relationships ended, Monica was devastated. Her strong, take-charge personality was reduced to a fragile wisp.

Peter, who had witnessed her pattern for years, told her that she was more dependent than she thought. She saw fragility as negative and sought to eradicate it at all costs. As a result, her vulnerability became unconscious, only to emerge in exaggerated form whenever she suffered the loss of a love: she would become dependent and clingy. Being faced with her dependence was particularly difficult for Monica, because her independence was such a central part of her identity. Getting a glimpse of her own shadow was so traumatic that it opened the door to the realm of the collective Shadow in her dreams. She fully enters that realm in the next section.

One must not get stuck here, needing to move instead through this block, just as if it were a creative block. It is often mirrored in our creative lives in just this way.

Stage Four: The Shadow Unmasked

Art is an attempt to integrate evil.
—*Simone de Beauvoir*

In this dream stage, we embody the shadow. Our situations in these dreams test us more than in any other kind of dream because they engage our souls in a time of despair. Dreams, here, often have a religious quality, drawing on the traditions of our own culture or more universal spiritual principles. In some of these dreams, we behave in ways that surprise and shock us: we did not know we were capable of such actions. As Monica learned, these dreams present us with the stark truth of our feelings.

Monica's third dream occurred two months after the second. The daughter of a Catholic father and an atheist mother, Monica did not identify herself with any particular religion, calling herself an agnostic. She did not believe in hell or demons:

DREAM THREE: I was in hell. I realized it suddenly. There was this stone building—crumbling ruins—ancient, and some kind of evil force. It was dark and windy. I began to say the Lord's Prayer. My eyes were closed. I couldn't look. I was absolutely terrified. I said the prayer, but I thought it didn't work. My voice rose in power and strength. At the end, I was shouting. Demons, vague and diaphanous, and somehow not quite real but still terrifying, disappeared one by one. When I opened my eyes, there were only a couple of people there "innocents," I thought. The demons were gone. I awoke, heart racing and panicked.

This dream was so powerful that Monica vividly recalls it several years later. She really was in a hellish realm at this time in her life, and the dream was a turning point for her. In it, Monica used her terror and courage to protect herself in a vulnerable situation. This dream showed her that she possessed both fragility and strength in her personality. By refusing to run, and thus placing herself at great risk, Monica learned that vulnerability requires strength. She felt humbled by her new insight about herself, and was less inclined to present herself as always being strong and independent.

The next dream shows Monica's ability to detach from, recognize, and observe the part of herself that must "die":

DREAM FOUR: A man is in my house, in my room, but I don't see him, just know he's going to do something— kill me. He is vaguely familiar and scary. He shoots himself eleven times, all over, to kill himself. He knows he must die. Someone, a woman, has been taking pictures of him while he shot himself. The middle one shows who he really is. He's evil. The devil. I know who he is, just before he dies.

In Monica's fifth dream, which she had a few weeks later, she found herself in the Shadowland, a landscape of despair that amplified her sense of hopelessness and reflected it back to her:

DREAM FIVE: I am walking all alone across a great field of cold lava. It is black in every direction, and flat, stretching as far as I can see, to the horizon. The sun is going down and the sky is a brilliant red. It is going to get very dark. The air is hot: I feel it going in my lungs as I breathe. I am on a paved road, narrow, curving through the lava. There is nothing living. Far off, against the horizon, I can just make out a single sapling. It will take me all night to get there. I can hear only my own footsteps. I keep walking.

Shadow contents have erupted into Monica's consciousness. She is alone, able at this point to recognize them as her own, and not just the characteristics of others. The landscape of her old self is dead. A new tree (a symbol of the self and of life) promises renewal and rebirth, but Monica realizes she has a long way to walk before reaching it.

Monica might have stopped her exploration early on, rationalizing Peter's comments as misguided. She might have remained stuck in believing that everyone else was weak and clingy, and continued to deny these qualities in herself. If she had done so, the pattern would have continued on. By being willing to unmask the shadow, no matter how painful, Monica gained great insight and, as we will see in the next chapter, released her creativity. At the end of this period, she was full of energy and inspiration. She began to write again and no longer felt attracted to those who undermined her talent.

We now leave the shadow realm and consider further the devils and witches who block us at this stage in our journey.

Frightening Soul Mates

He [the animus] personifies brutality, coldness, and
obstinancy and paralyzes a woman's growth.
—Marie-Louise von Franz

As Monica began to confront personal shadow qualities in her dreams, she was confronted with the more powerful and frightening collective Shadow. In the most dramatic and transformative of these dreams, a demon appeared. The Western collective image of masculine evil is the devil, and the feminine equivalent image is the wicked witch. These figures appear in our dreams when we are facing the deepest, most unconscious, and potentially transformative qualities within. These qualities are so unknown and so far away from our consciousness that, as with animals and strangers, we perceive them as being other than us. In our dreams they are often embodied by the opposite of our physical selves—the opposite sex.

This was true of Michael's dream, which occurred a few weeks after the last dream of his father:

> I dreamed I was with a man, a stranger. We were play-
> ing some game. He was showing it to me. There were
> these women who thought they knew that other people
> were bad. The women were witches and they would
> grab someone from their house and just kill them. They
> believed they were doing the right thing. The man with
> me was explaining both sides to me.

The collection of our most unknown and unacknowledged qualities are called the *anima* and *animus*.[86] The anima refers to all of
those characteristics about ourselves that are feminine (yin, or inner
woman), whereas the animus holds all of our masculine (yang, or
inner man) qualities. Feminine and masculine do not refer to cul-
tural gender stereotypes. Rather, only those qualities that would be
considered masculine or feminine in all cultures, across time, are
contained by the anima and animus. In chapter 3, we discovered that
people who create tend to be more psychologically androgynous
than other people, to express both masculine and feminine characteristics in their personalities. They are able to integrate the animus
(action and intellect) with the anima (receptivity and emotionality)
in their creative work. This continually requires them to become
aware of those unknown qualities within, in order to feed their creativity. Typically, women express the anima in their lives and are less
in touch with the animus, whereas men express the animus and are
less in touch with the anima. What we are less in touch with within
ourselves gets embodied and expressed in our dreams. It also tends
to get projected outward onto other real people in the world. We
come to know ourselves by interacting with others and learning to
tell the difference between who they really are, and who we are.

As we become consciously aware of these anima and animus qualities within us, the figures who represent them in our dreams become more familiar and personal as well as more positive, just as our shadow figures do. The ways in which the shadow and the anima and animus differ is in their content: the shadow holds qualities of which we can become conscious much more easily than we can those of the anima and animus. The latter are more foreign to us and, therefore, more threatening. The anima and animus also provide a link to our spiritual nature, being the inner figures who help us find a sense of meaning and purpose. As such, they lead us to become whole. We become attracted to those who represent our less familiar anima or animus qualities. For example, we all remember the stereotypical high school pairing of the fluffy cheerleader and the macho football player. He embodied her disowned strength and aggressiveness, while she represented for him his opposite.

In addition to being unfamiliar, anima and animus figures, as they appear in our dreams, also reflect our personality development. The table on page 176 provides characteristics associated with each level of the anima and animus as they develop within us. It can help us identify how aware we are of our own anima and animus qualities. Each of these stages has a positive and a negative pole, and the images evoked by each stage are exaggerated and stereotypical. Remember that what makes them "good" or "bad" depends upon what the figures do with the quality, and upon our own value judgments about them. The more we resist acknowledging a quality within us, the more negative the figure can seem. We all need each one of these qualities at one time or another:[87]

STAGES OF THE ANIMA AND ANIMUS

STAGE ONE	Biological woman or temptress, woman of the body. Represents sex, attraction, motherhood (Eve, Delilah)	Man of physical power and strength (Sampson, Goliath)
STAGE TWO	Cultivated, intelligent woman; spiritual companion (Helen of Troy, Cleopatra)	Man of action and initiative (Achilles, Attila the Hun)
STAGE THREE	Spiritual, virtuous woman (the Virgin Mary, Joan of Arc)	Intellectual, man of words (Winston Churchill, Rasputin)
STAGE FOUR	Wise woman (Mother Theresa, evil witch)	Wise man (Gandhi, Satan)

The animus figures in Monica's dreams develop across her series. In her first dream, the man with the hypodermic who threatened her friend was a stage one animus figure, representing a quality about herself that she was just beginning to become aware of. In her second dream, Peter is a positive animus figure who is determined to act to save her friend, representing stage two. The stage three negative animus (the mad scientists holding her friend) seems less evil than that in the first dream: she is becoming more aware of "his" qualities within her. In her third dream, Monica's stage four negative animus is a group of demons, certainly evil and powerful, but also not quite real. In her fourth dream, the animus figure becomes familiar and loses his power to harm her. In this dream, the death is a positive one; part of her needed to die in order to be recognized and integrated into her self-concept—to die. Remember that in dreams, death is not always negative. It can represent the need for an old, outgrown, perhaps self-destructive part of ourselves to die so that new growth can occur, as it did in Michael's dream of his father dying.

In a previous chapter, we explored Devon's dream of a dark-haired child whom her mother loved, which reflected back her mother's continuing, negative influence on her creativity. As Devon came closer to transforming an old pattern, she later dreamed of shadow figures and a stage four negative animus—Satan:

> I am with a group of women, witches of some sort. We go to a meadow near my childhood house. We join hands in a large ring; there are many such rings. We sing and run around our rings. There is a storm. We see waves, huge waves with sharp peaks. The water is beautiful—turquoise and deep blue. I realize Satan is coming, engineering the apocalypse. This knowledge dawns on me calmly and the rings are doing all they can to prevent it. They seem joyous and not apprehensive. Next, I see a man I know who is trying to help me by telling me he saw an angelfish in the waves, a huge red angelfish. It was the seventh angelfish. I somehow know this is the seventh angel of the apocalypse. The fish holds all of the DNA of all living things on earth. It must be saved for after the apocalypse. Then I am with my mother. I know that Satan has possessed people. He's on the move, creating the end of the world. My mother and I are in a car and she is driving. She says we're going to take a little detour, with a sly, sneaking, evil look at me. It is absolutely horrifying, even now. I know she's been taken. I turn and leap out of the car. I don't belong there.

This dream is loaded with religious symbols and archetypes. Notice also that it contains many of the elements we explored in parts I and II of this book: weather, water, obstacles, emotion, animals, and a vehicle. It also continues the main theme of Devon's dream series, but adds hopefulness and a helpful dream character.

In the next chapter, we will meet more helpful dream characters—positive shadow or anima and animus figures, including the wise old man in Monica's dreams, who helps her express all that she has gained from her inner explorations in her creative work.

Treading the Path with Care

As mentioned in chapter 8, shadow-searching can be dangerous. Prominent creative people, having had difficult childhoods and being more sensitive to their environments than others, have a greater chance of becoming depressed. Suicidal feelings are often the outcome of one part of the self's wishing to destroy another part. An attacking anima or animus figure might also besiege us. We become confused, identifying ourselves with the shadow, unable to see the rest of our psyche through the darkness cast by our despair. Believing this is all we are, we may want to destroy ourselves.

It is at this point, which can last for an unendurably long time, that we must be most vigilant and courageous. Must we really murder our own selves? Or might we need to destroy (by becoming aware of) a self-destructive part of our personalities in order to grow and become more creative?

Long-standing patterns in our lives are best confronted with the aid of a psychologist skilled in negotiating the often treacherous territory of the psyche. If you experience frightening or painful emotions or feel overwhelmed while working with your dreams, please seek help immediately! The days are gone when to ask for help was considered a weakness. Psychotherapy has been a rite of passage for many creative people before you.[88] Visit my website for more helpful suggestions: www.drtonay.com.

In the next chapter, we will turn toward dream figures who offer aid or comfort, and discover how they can provide us with more keys to unlock our creativity.

◇ ≈ ◇ ≈ ◇

Frantically, you search the pockets of your cloak, seeking anything that might help you get through the wall. You find your Rilke parchment, quill pen, and the green gem. You take a step and feel a crunch beneath your shoe. Reaching down, you find a cracked mirror. It is oval shaped, fashioned from dark green stone, with a small ground indentation on the handle where your gem just might fit. Remembering the pond, you hesitate before looking at yourself in the mirror. You read the quote again for courage and hold the mirror directly in front of your face. You blink as your face changes from wicked, evil sorcerer to ugly wretch, to horrible beast, and back again. This time, you do not flinch. You have seen it all before, and clearly. These are parts of myself, and they are not particularly flattering, *you think.* But that makes me no better or worse than anyone else. And some of them might even be useful. *You shudder to think of the ways in which you have judged others with qualities so similar to your newly discovered ones.*

Vowing to transform these characteristics through your creative work, you gently place the gem in the handle of the mirror. Nothing happens. The gatekeeper returns, but after considering what you have already been through, you find you are no longer afraid.

"I have no key with which to open the door," you say, boldly. "I have only these things: pen, mirror, parchment, and myself. Please let me pass."

The gatekeeper regards you carefully, eyes sparkling while spying the handle of the mirror. "Ah...to pass will cost you the gem."

You remember how you nearly lost the jewel at the river and had to confront the beast to get it back. Now, you understand that it offered you comfort and protection. Realizing you no longer need these things, you hand the gatekeeper the glowing gem. Instantly, the lock pops open with a ping. Beyond the door, the land stretches out before you into a great circular clearing. You thank the gatekeeper and step, blinking, into the sunlight. . .

Chapter 10

Guides and Lovers: Those Who Help Us Find Our Way

Creative people knock on silence for an answering music;
they pursue meaninglessness until they can force it to mean.
—*Rollo May*

WHEN WE CAST A LIGHT into the dark spaces of our souls, we illuminate shadows. When creating, we court shadow and, by doing so, release our creativity. In our dreams, the forms of the shadow— whether animals, strangers, or people we know—are elusive and often frightening, but they can also be unexpectedly friendly and helpful.

When you dream of helpful strangers, you can rest assured there is a part of yourself ready to aid you. Your willingness to be helped is probably being reflected in the outside world, too, where you may find yourself feeling less isolated and more a part of a community (as you will find in the next chapter).

In this chapter, you will meet dream figures who often appear in your dreams after you have crossed the broken bridge of intense emotion, reexperienced feelings from the past, and delved into our inner depths, being faced with unpleasant parts of yourself. By the time you experience such helpful dreams, you already know the ways in which to unlock your creativity; but you need reminding and encouragement as you begin to change your old ways. Your dream characters now lead you toward the next step in our creative expression, helping you through the most stubborn of obstacles, or accompanying you to supportive witnesses on your journey, reminding you of where you have been.

As you saw in part II, those elements and themes you discovered earlier in the book recur in your dreams as you progress on your spiraling path of creative self-discovery. Watch for the themes of loss, children, and natural obstacles, the shadow, and anima and animus as you read through the dreams presented in this chapter.

Helpful Shadows:
Witnessing How Far We Have Come

Art is the only thing that can go on mattering once it has stopped hurting.
—*Elizabeth Bowen*

In this section, we look at dreams in which others travel with us, offering no direct help, but lending a sense of support. We may wake from these dreams feeling pensive and quiet, surprised at how real and familiar this person seemed within our dreams.

Isabel Allende dreams of her grandmother when her writing is going well.[89] Her grandmother offers her a sense of being protected. In these dreams, the author simply watches her grandmother writing and feels soothed. Taking the outward path perspective, the author's real grandmother probably had a calming effect on her. The older woman died when Isabel Allende was quite young, and perhaps the author's memories of her grandmother are those of a child being comforted by a wise and creative woman. The inward path unveils a helpful, positive shadow figure, which is reflected in the ways in which her grandmother has become part of her and lives on within her. Such dreams are lovely and numinous, staying with us long after we wake up, and providing inspiration and encouragement for our creative work. Isabel Allende's dream honors her grandmother and herself, and offers the author the sense that she is on the right path.

In chapter 6, we explored this house-dream of a journalist:

> I am in my childhood house. I had moved out. I went back to pick up a few things I'd left and needed. I got there and there was tons of junk. I started in my room and threw most of it away. I didn't need this stuff anymore. It was an overwhelming task.

This later dream returns to the scene of the first and adds a helpful shadow figure:

> I was in my childhood backyard with the aim of digging up a small, new tree to take home. I was with two other— men. I found a little plant among several. All I had was a Popsicle™ stick, so I drew a wide circle around the tree, cutting through old, dead grass. The stump of the old tree was nearby. Just then, I saw someone come through the front door—the new owner. She seemed to know me when I introduced myself. She showed us the house, which was much nicer, larger, and completely remodeled. It had been under construction for some time. She was very warm, saying she wanted to show me this so that I would realize I no longer live here.

Consider the house in this dream, the tree, and the dream characters. Comparing it to the earlier dream, the dreamer could see the progress of her creative development. Not only is there now a helpful shadow figure, but there are also two characters of the opposite sex helping her bring the tree of the self home. These animus figures actively guide her toward herself.

Inner Guides and the Path to the Soul

The anima is the mover, the instigator of change, whose fascination drives, lures, and encourages the male to all the adventures of the soul and spirit, of action and creation in the inner and the outward world.

—*Erich Neumann*[90]

[The animus] gives the woman spiritual firmness, and invisible inner support...On this highest level the inner man acts as a bridge to the Self. He personifies a woman's capacities of courage, spirit and truth and connects her to the source of her personal creativity.

—*Marie-Louise von Franz*[91]

As we found in the last chapter, the anima and animus in dreams lead us to the heart of our creative spirit, to the deepest and most genuine parts of ourselves, and help us become whole. Just as in your encounters with the shadow, your task is to meet, accept, and acknowledge the qualities represented by anima and animus dream figures, and by so doing, change them from negative (unknown) to positive (known). As prominent Jungian analyst Marie-Louise von Franz said, "To transform [them] involves immense suffering, for it means nothing less than forsaking an old identity for a new one. It takes a great deal of courage. But the journey is well undertaken, for the rewards are immeasurable."[92]

Although negative anima and animus dreams can be among our most terrifying, helpful anima and animus dream figures frequently awaken us with a sense of well-being and joy. Sometimes these dreams seem to be saying all is well, and others guide us.

To illustrate how these dream characters can help us, we return to three of Chris's dreams from chapter 1:

DREAM ONE: I was at an awards presentation with R. [familiar woman]. An admiral [some man] came up to me and gave me a ring that had a little steel ball in it. If you shook the ring, the little steel ball would roll around and make a chiming sound. The admiral asked me to join the Navy.

DREAM THREE: I feel lost. My brother, Richard, is there. He tells me I don't have the right books and helps me get the right ones. An old friend, D. [familiar woman], is also there, and helps me get what I need.

DREAM FOUR: I'm in some kind of rickety theater. Phil Donahue [talk show host] is backstage. He is holding a baby [one of my cousins, a girl] who is crying. I run in there because a group of some men [strangers] are trying to beat me up. I hold the baby and rock it to sleep. I follow Mr. Donahue to his house, but he doesn't want me to...The guys find me. I ask them who they are...They beat me up and leave. I go to Donahue's house. He says I can stay and he will help me.

These dreams illustrate that Chris is becoming more aware of the positive animus. In the first dream, a powerful, unfamiliar authority figure invites her to join him. In the second, the helpful animus figure is a familiar relative. The third dream contains both a positive, now-familiar animus figure and a negative, unfamiliar one (the group of men). Unfortunately, that dream indicates that she must first get "beaten up" by the negative animus in order for the positive animus (who protects her creativity in the form of the baby) to emerge and aid her.

In applying this dream to her life, Chris might consider, as have other dreamers in this book, what happens in her life and within her mind when she begins to create. Becoming aware of negative, inner forces helps us identify, observe, and, eventually, transform them. Is it possible for Chris to create without beating herself up?

Giselle, the young dancer-choreographer from chapter 1, had a dream in which a positive masculine figure illuminated a paradox in a time of trouble. This dream contains many other elements we explored in other chapters:

> In my hands, I am holding a putty ball, an egg, a child. It is a child, but it is cupped in my small white hand, a soft pink ball of putty the size of an egg. I carry her through the winding streets of Jerusalem to all the corners, everywhere. She is so soft, I can't catch her, and she falls to the ground. When I reach to retrieve her, a piece is missing. She falls apart as she rolls on the ground. Putty is dripping through my fingers. I have no control.
>
> "Here," I say, presenting the melted egg to her father. "I'm sorry," I say, turning away.
>
> "Had she melted into the cracks of any other city I could not thank you more," he said.
>
> I turn back to face him and I see a child, wider than most, full and fat from that egg, from that gooey piece of nothing, and here she is, smiling and fat. She looks like a combination of Z. [family friend] and M. [my cousin], with dark hair. I gather her in my arms and feel the warmth that can only be given by a child, and I become lost in thoughts of motherhood and how children in my life sometimes fill my emptiness...

Within the dream, Giselle initially saw the loss of the formless egg—all potential—as negative. The animus sees it differently: he knows of the possibility for transformation and growth. By melting into a supremely spiritual place in Giselle's religious tradition, the egg transforms into a robust child, who gives Giselle feelings of warmth and fullness. The animus figure may be advising Giselle to embrace her spirituality in order to actualize her creative potential.

Exercise: Coming to Know the Animus / Anima

1) Recall a dream in which you encountered a compelling opposite sex character who acted as a guide or helper. This exercise is best done with a positive dream figure.

2) In a quiet place where you will be uninterrupted, imagine yourself walking into a simple room in the middle of a forest, or other natural environment. The dream character will enter from a door at the opposite side. Imagine the character entering.

3) Thank the character for appearing, and ask his or her name. Ask whether it is all right for you to ask a few questions. Wait quietly for the answer. (Don't feel silly; this is a technique called active imagination, which is very useful for working with dream figures.) Ask the character about him or herself, impressions of you, and advice for your creative work.

4) Make sure you thank the character when you are finished, and ask if you may visit again.

5) Ask questions of your anima or animus figure whenever you are creatively blocked, confused, or disheartened. Often, they offer keys to the way through. In this way, you are opening a dialogue between your conscious and unconscious, which helps encourage creativity and provides inspiration.

Sexual Encounters

In chapter 3, we discovered that, seeming to contradict the old Freudian notion that people who create are wild cauldrons of libidinous energy flinging sexuality around like drops of paint off a brush, people who create may have slightly less sexuality overall in dreams than average.

But less does not imply absence. On average, sexuality occurs in one in twenty-five dreams of women, and one in ten dreams of men.[93] It may be more frequently reported now in women's dreams than it was in the past.[94] Those occasions when you do dream about sex are most likely to occur when you are working creatively during the day.

There are many theories about sexuality in our dream lives. Freud felt sexual dreams represent an unconscious wish for or fear of sex: for instance, a dream of having sex with someone meant you wished, in your deepest, darkest self, to have sex with that person.[95]

Jung believed that dream sexuality mirrors the blending of masculine and feminine that occurs within one's own psyche,[96] representing two parts of the self joining together and integrating: the anima and animus. In fact, sexual encounters with anima and animus figures are among the most powerful dreams.

People who create do tend to be more psychologically androgynous, blending masculine (active, expressive) and feminine (receptive, intuitive) attitudes in their personalities and behavior, using both while creating. I found that, although sometimes we do have sexual dreams of people we secretly wish to have sex with, our sexual dreams more often represent a blending of elements within the psyche that were previously unexpressed or unacknowledged. Sexual dreams are therefore very important to the creative dreamer, because what we are blending and unifying within often finds its expression without.

Writer John Nichols reported this intense sexual dream, which he eventually used in a novel:

> . . . a very erotic dream of being inside a kind of bubble or a placenta, floating through what was apparently outer space with a woman I did not know. It seems like most of the erotic dreams that I've had in my life are with people that I don't know. Just total strangers. That's kind of curious to me. This was a total stranger. I was just floating in this kind of bubble, wanting very desperately to make love, but not being able to because any kind of sharp or passionate movement might rend a tear in the placenta-bubble and let in a vacuum. It was a tremendously erotic dream because I had to withhold. The woman that I was with really wanted to make love.

> She kept pushing and pushing. I was terrified to actually
> generate that kind of passion or action for fear of tear-
> ing the bubble.[97]

There are elements of this dream that illustrate principles we have explored. First, the dreamer is struck by the fact that most of his sexual dream encounters are with strangers. As we learned in chapter 1, it is perfectly common for men to dream mostly of strangers—men's sexual dream interactions are usually with unfamiliar partners. From an inward path view, Nichols is coming in contact with the unfamiliar, unacknowledged, feminine qualities within his own psyche, the anima, that would like to join with him, despite his fear. He may be afraid that getting close will "burst his bubble" (the illusion) of love. Nichols calls his enclosure a "placenta-bubble," a place where new life is created. If the bubble bursts, all that is left is a vacuum (emptiness). Viewed this way, Nichols's dream could teach him that he may be resisting his feminine side for fear that expressing it will destroy his creativity and leave him empty.

However, Nichols was also having heart problems at the time of the dream. The dream may simply have presented him with the extent of his fear about his very real medical condition (outward path), or both interpretations (middle path) may have been appropriate. Each dream has many possible interpretations, as psychologist Alfred Adler observed when describing the several possible meanings of a test-taking dream:

> With some individuals the meaning of such dreams
> would be: "You are not prepared to face the problem
> before you." With others it would mean: "You have

passed examinations before, and you will pass the present test also." One individual's symbols are never the same as another's. What we must consider chiefly in the dream is the residue of mood and its coherence with the whole style of life."[98]

This is why it is important to look at a whole series of your dreams, rather than just one or two, to identify patterns of meaningful themes. Interpreting a series of dreams is a far more reliable way of discerning your creative conflicts and strengths.

Lydia, a painter in her forties, dreamed of an unfamiliar man who, although she had no real interaction with him, reflected her growing awareness of her masculine qualities and integration of them into her self-concept. From the outward path, we might suspect she wishes to or plans to have an affair. The inward path sees the man as a reflection of the emerging animus, or masculine aspects.

A friend and I get calls from men we don't know. (I'm married in real life.) They're supposed to be blind dates. . . . Finally, I talk to hers again and decide to meet him. At first he's not good-looking, kind of lanky. But after I look and talk to him, I notice he's quite good-looking. He's got a beautiful body and his hair is long, thick, and dark, and I decide he's of French origin.

Now I'm putting this man's hair into individual ponytails. It seems as if his hair was quite thick until I pulled it into these ponytails. Then I could see his scalp. It didn't look good at all. At this point, his hair becomes mine. I incorporate his hair! I decide to take it out of the ponytails and let it hang loose. It looks really good. There was a sexual feeling connected to him.

At the end of the dream, she feels sexual, another sign that she is beginning to "join with" these hitherto unknown aspects of herself, as they have become part of her changing self-image.

~~~~~~~~~~~~~~~~~~~~~~

Exercise: Sexual Dreams

Sift through your dream journal for any sexual dreams you have had. A sexual dream is one that contains sexual thoughts and feelings, not just kissing, fondling, or other more obvious sexual behaviors.

1) In the space below, list the characters for whom you expressed desire in your dreams. Then, write as much as you can about each one. What kind of people are they? What are their personalities like? How would they most enjoy an afternoon? In conversation, what topics would interest them? What type of creative expression would they enjoy? If you are observing a sexual interaction between two other characters, describe each of them.

_____

_____

_____

_____

_____

2) Do you see any similarities? The qualities you described comprise the anima or animus, your own unknown masculine or feminine side. Ask people who know you well if they have seen these aspects of yourself, and when. Try exhibiting these characteristics consciously, just as you did with your shadow qualities. As you do so, you will be integrating them so that they can be better put to use in your creative life.

Intimations of Wholeness: The Mandala

In chapter 8 and earlier in this chapter, we met Devon, who had left an Ivy League academic career, which her mother would have preferred for her, to become a freelance graphic artist. As she remained firm in her commitment to her creative life, faced emotional rejection from her mother (the pain of the reality of their relationship), and gained self-insight, Devon's dream world transformed. In these two illuminating dreams, Devon is accompanied by the animus, comfortable with feelings and with herself. Compare these dreams with the shadow and negative animus figures in the dream on page 177:

> DREAM ONE: A man and I were at the beach. I've never really been to this beach. It had golden light and natural rock formations. He was diving in the ocean. It was warm. I was on the shore, then waded in, looking at beautiful shells. Then I walked over to a rock with many

crystals growing within it. They were all colors. Bright, vibrant, pastel, all sizes and shapes. There was one, pink and blue, beautiful colors. I dug it out of the rock.

DREAM TWO: I was in Europe in the ocean near the shore and a huge rock formation. It was incredibly beautiful, sienna-colored with white veins running through, shaded. The lines were intricate. There were many people there, women, some children. A man was on the other side of the rocks, in the water, further than me, beckoning me onward. I knew it was safe, something about him felt so comfortable, so I ventured out. I floated on my back, very buoyant, in the clear water. I climbed onto a rock to get to the other side. I looked more closely at the rock. Many small pieces fitted intricately together to make up the whole. I wanted to pry the most beautiful piece loose to give to the man. It was perfectly symmetrical, incredible to look at. I was indebted to him for something, very grateful.

Devon's dreams are the positive equivalent of the stage four shadow dream, in which we dream of a stark landscape, feeling a spiritual and emotional void. In these dreams, Devon finds a symmetrical, balanced object. It is a mandala, the symbol of the Self integrated and whole. Mandalas are often circular and can be found in all cultures' spiritual artwork, and many of them are illustrated in Jung's classic book, *Man and His Symbols.*[99] Jung observed when working with psychotic, severely disturbed patients, that their artwork and dreams contained mandalas, which moved from fragmentation toward wholeness during the course of a psychotic episode.[100] The state of the mandala echoes the state of the psyche.[101]

When creating, we re-form ourselves in the course of our work. To produce, we transform not only our ideas, but also our very selves. Seeking mandala images in your dreams can help you see where you are in the process of moving toward wholeness.

The last dreamer to whom we return is Monica (the writer who was confronted with her dependency by her ex), whose archetypal stage three and four dreams we explored in the last chapter. No longer trying to save shadow figures from the hell realm, Monica is accompanied by a helpful, archetypal wise old man in this haunting dream in which she seeks a mandala:

> I was walking through a misty, grassy graveyard, ancient and British. I had gone through the gate, crossed the grass, straight to a huge stone. A very old man was behind me in the mist. He emanated a powerful presence, and I instinctively knew he was strong and gentle at the same time. He knew exactly who he was. As he gazed at me, I felt he knew everything about me, knew why I was here. His eyes moved toward the stone. *He knew where to find it all along,* I thought. It was like the end of a kind of quest, and I hadn't much time. It was of tremendous importance. I pick up the stone. It was a square, a couple of feet high with markings on each of its four corners, down the side. They were black or carved deeply on a gray surface. Ancient markings, like hieroglyphics. I brought the stone to a wood-paneled room full of people. I was going to reveal the secret of the stone. I was waiting for the light to shine through the window and illuminate its face. I saw it was a sort of clock with no hands, but had Roman numerals

carved around the circular edge. The numeral I was the key to everything.

When Monica learned that the stone she sought was a mandala, she immediately connected the Roman numeral I with the word "I." It seemed crucial to understanding the dream's meaning. She felt it was the most important dream she had ever had. Monica was desperate to remember the markings on the stone.

After a time, Monica thought that perhaps she already knew the meaning of the dream—the point was to find the stone, and she had already done that. The stone contained ancient wisdom, insight beyond words. She brought it to the world to share it with others. Monica had traveled the landscape of her dreams and her past in order to come to know and accept herself. Only then was she able to reveal the "I" honestly and without fear. Only then was she able to express who she really was to others who could value and support her creativity. Her self-insight gave genuineness and depth to her character and, as a writer, to her characters as well. Her fiction no longer mirrored the life pattern that had been holding her back for so long. Her plots changed, becoming more complex and real. Monica felt full of energy and finally prepared to live the creative life.

The dream of the stone emerging from a graveyard of the past contrasted so strongly with her earlier dreams that it helped her see how far she had come, and to recognize that no matter what happens in her outer life, she now has a wise and helpful companion within to help orient her toward the "I" when she loses her sense of self.

Exercise: Creating a Symbol of Wholeness

Mandalas are ancient depictions of our state of integration. As we create, we call upon all aspects of ourselves to bring into being something new. In this exercise, you will want to look through your dream journal for a mandala image: a symmetrical, balanced object, often a square or circle (such as the sun, moon, or earth). Once you have found it, make a sketch of it. Are there ways you could elaborate it, including images within it to represent parts of yourself, your creative life, and people you love?

Consider making a creative product of your own mandala. You may want to do this alone, or gather your community around you, with all of you creating garden stepping-stones, medallions, or paintings, or even communicating aspects of your mandala through movement or dance. Some people sketch mandalas in their dream journals and are delighted at how they change over time.

Exercise: How Far We Have Come

This next dream of Giselle's (the dancer-choreographer who dreamed of the melting egg) should sound familiar, for it was the dream that opened this book. In it, we find almost all of the elements we explored in earlier chapters. Without reading what you wrote about it when you first began to read *The Creative Dreamer,* reconsider the dream that follows. At the end of the dream is a worksheet where you can write your reflections about the elements and themes you learned about in previous chapters. By so doing, you will learn how far you have come since setting out upon the creative path of dreams.

Giselle's striking and complex dream chronicles her creative journey:

> An acquaintance I knew ran by me and a group, screaming and holding her head. "Get me out! I need to leave! Get me out of here!" She ran into the woods. We decided we had to help her, so we all ran after her, but we came to the edge of the sea. She had gone to the other side and the only way we could get there was to cross the water. We got in and started inching across using these handles that were attached to a wall. We moved across slowly, hand by hand, as if we were children in a beginning swimming class, scared of the water. The water started swelling and violently moving—we were scared of drowning. I suddenly grew very impatient. The people in front of me were going too slow. I began to move very fast, passing them up, trying to keep my head above the waves since I had to let go of the handles to pass them.
>
> I got to the other side, and when I got out (I was in a place that looked like the Old City of Jerusalem), everything was made of stone. I walked and eventually came to a doctor's office. I asked about Sharon, the woman who had run by us, screaming. They said the doctor was seeing her and I should wait. I looked around and saw a little brown dog on a chair. It was lying on its back and its whole front side, neck to abdomen, was cut open, the

skin pulled back and its organs sat neatly inside. I distinctly remember its two front paws, they were bent and playing with its insides. I reached over and pulled out the heart. It was wrapped in Saran Wrap and it was beating…I bought something to eat. People kept telling me how dangerous and unclean it was for me to eat food while I was holding this beating heart. I began a very intricate eating pattern, the food and the heart were rolling on my fingers, and I had to move my hands to keep them from falling or touching.

It began to get dark and I realized I needed to get back. I began running, clutching my food and the heart tightly. I didn't know how to get back. An old woman with a young son started running next to me. We were all hunched over, legs bent, running as if we were ducking from something. We began to race each other. I stopped suddenly. A long, empty stone road was before me. No people, just darkness and moonlight. I saw, way in the distance, Leah, a woman I'd worked with for two weeks on an archeological dig. She was squatting on the road, and as I looked at her, she pointed her finger in the direction I should go and a glowing green light indicated the distance. It grew out of her finger like those light saber swords from *Star Wars*.

Listed in the worksheet are several creative dream elements we discussed in other chapters. Read back through Giselle's dream. On the left, briefly describe the element as it occurs in the dream. On the right, write a few short phrases to remind you of what the element might indicate about Giselle and her creativity.

WORKSHEET: GISELLE'S DREAM

ELEMENTS	PHRASES
Emotions	
Earth, Air, Fire, Water	
Children	
Loss	
Illness, Physical Problems	
Natural Obstacles	
Endangered Others	
Animals	
Threatening Others	
Helpful Shadow or Anima and Animus Figures	
Mandalas	

Now consider all of the elements as a whole. What does this dream indicate about Giselle's creative process? First, note the feeling tone of the dream. What emotions are being expressed that may give Giselle insight into feelings she needs to experience more fully?

Looking at the story line of the dream, what obstacles must Giselle overcome to get to where she is headed? Asking the three key questions from chapter 8 may help:

KEY QUESTIONS WORKSHEET

ELEMENTS	PHRASES
Threat	
What Dreamer Did	
Did It Work?	

In the end, what significance does Leah hold for the dreamer? You might want to interpret this dream from first the outward, then the inward, path. Consider how both perspectives could simultaneously be true. In this way, you will reach the middle path.

The Creative Dance

Our creative, spiritual, and emotional lives are inextricably linked as one mirrors the others, reflecting ourselves back to ourselves, and marking our changes as we progress on the ever-spiraling creative path. The journey is perilous, often painful, and always challenging. What we bring back to our creative lives from this inner adventure is precious: the keys with which to unlock our creativity.

We leave this chapter of helpful dream characters with a dream from Nevin, the creative man from chapter 8 who needed to learn to stop turning back when confronted with others who block his way. This dream eloquently portrays the movements of our inner selves as we come to know, accept, and bring what was unknown and in shadow into the light:

> On stage, in a center spotlight aimed downward, is a dancer, dancer one. The dancer is moving sadly as if in a confined space. Soon, another dancer, dancer two, comes in from the dark. Two crawls over one, their bodies parallel. When hands meet and knees meet, they begin to move in unison. Their movements reflect a relationship, quiet and searching and joyful. They move only within the light and are always touching and always mirroring each other's actions. After some time, they end up in the same position as when they first met, but now two is below and one is on top. They pause, they detach, one leaves the light. Two, after a pause, begins to move with similar movements that one had when alone. Lights dim.

◻ ≈ ◻ ≈ ◻

How strange it feels to be in the sunlight again. The warmth holds back the chill of the dark wood that surrounds you. As you emerge into the clearing, you notice the sounds of the place. Once again, birds sing, dragonflies buzz by, and an eagle calls as it glides freely above you. There are no pools here for looking into. Relieved, you sigh. You walk to the center of this perfectly circular space. Your senses seem sharper here. Everything looks vibrant with color and form. The sun's warmth has opened wildflowers, and their scents, all mixed together, scramble over one another to meet you. Here in the center is a mound of stones, and within them a spring bubbles forth. A few errant leaves make their way down the diminutive stream and over the miniature waterfalls before heading back underground.

You smile and look about you for a container. Alas, there is none and you doubt whether you could take the water with you, anyway. Instead, you cup your hands and fill them, drinking of the smooth liquid. Ah! A sensation like the ringing of soft chimes moves through your mind. You shake your head a bit. You feel completely clear. With nothing to stop you, within or without, you eagerly head out of the clearing and back home. You are filled with energy, ready to bring all that you have gained with you to create. But how do you get out of here? And how will you ever find your way back?

Just then, a figure approaches, seemingly appearing from the air. It is the gatekeeper, grown old and careful and slow. The gatekeeper nods, eyes gleaming. "You have done well. You have truly earned the key to the forest." The gatekeeper pulls from a pocket a glowing gem. It is your green jewel! You smile as it is placed into your hand.

But what is to be done with it? *you wonder. . .*

≈ Chapter 11 ≈

Creative Community: The Return

What do we live for, if it is not to make life less difficult for each other?
—*George Eliot*

WHICHEVER PATH YOU HAVE CHOSEN, you have brought your dreams and arrived here in the clearing. You are alone, you are confronted with a riddle, and you do not know the answer. At certain points in the creative journey, you need help. It may come in the form of reflection on your work by others, or as emotional support from friends, family, a colleague, a manager, or an agent, or even from your own inner world.

In this chapter, you discover new ways of unlocking your creativity through your connection with yourself and with others, and consider the challenges you face when seeking to give and receive nourishing friendship. You explore ways to expand your community that will continually nourish your creativity. Then, you revisit the places you traveled in preparation for the return to the beginning…

Friends from the Forest

I don't know where it is, it seems like a small town with nice, just above modest, houses. I seem to know the area very well and feel quite at home there. As I say, not ecstatic, but comfortable.[102]

Maya Angelou dreams this dream when her work is going well. It reflects a place inside of her psyche where she is welcome and at ease. We usually think of communities as residing outside of ourselves, but we can have inner companions as well.

In this last part of the book, we explored the deepest regions of dreaming: those dreams where we are faced with the shadow, questions of existential meaning and spirituality, and the collective dark side. We found that when we are touched by despair, we are often closest to breaking through an old self-destructive pattern or shattering an outdated image of ourselves. When we stay with the emotion evoked in our dreams, follow it to its source, and connect it with our waking lives, changes can occur. Strange and helpful dream characters emerge to point the way forward, warn us of an impending slip backward, or simply encourage us and show us how far we have come. Some of our dreams can be truly inspiring and reviving, as is this reoccurring dream of Maurice Sendak's:

> I often recollect dreams of finding stationery stores, or what we called candy stores when I was a kid. They're excavating and they find a Brooklyn candy store intact behind ancient brick walls. It's opened up and there it is—the whole ambience of a thirties store. The women working in it are all thirties-dressed and hair doed, looking like Myrna Loy. Everything is just as it was when I was a child. All the beautiful toys are in their original boxes. There's this overwhelming joy at finding them.[103]

Once we reach this stage in our creative journey, we can turn to our dream figures for support when we become muddled and uncertain.

One way to do this is to ask ourselves a question before going to sleep, and then carefully consider our dreams in the morning. Several dream workers have written of techniques for incubating dreams.[104] The essential steps are to specify the question or problem as precisely as possible before falling asleep, preferably in writing, avoiding questions for which there could be a "yes" or "no" answer. Then, upon waking, regard the dream as if it were an answer to the question or problem, noting any associations or feelings evoked by the various elements and images in the dream. Although a dream cannot produce an answer itself (we must be conscious to do that!), it can make clear what we already know.

The most common problem those who create face in their work is being blocked. Throughout this book, we have approached that frustrating experience from many points of view. The journey through the forest moved us from the outer world of people and facts to the inner world of feelings, memories, and ideas, allowing us to meet, unmask, and work through our creative blocks. In the process, we found that our blocks are really symptoms of something within that needs recognition and expression, and without it, will not let us move forward.

In the last few chapters, we met inner, helpful dream figures who might offer yet another way to unlock our creativity by appearing in our incubated dreams and guiding us to the "something within" that needs our attention. Our inner helpmates can also ease our sense of loneliness and isolation while we create. I know artists and writers who regularly spend a few moments visiting their inner figures. Imagining our inner landscape and those who dwell there puts us back in touch with ourselves and can lend a sense of calm and confidence to the rest of our waking lives. If you find yourself becoming blocked or feeling alone, make an imaginary pilgrimage to the clearing in the forest and invite the gatekeeper to tea.

Exercise: Inner Figures and Dream Incubation

For this exercise, you will need no dreams from the past, only a notebook, something with which to write, your dream journal, and sleep. This exercise should be used sparingly, and only when you are experiencing a problem with your creativity: feeling extremely frustrated with your creative work; in the throes of a creative block; unsure about whether or not you want to continue; or feeling stuck and in need of a new direction for your project. Fold a sheet of paper in half lengthwise, or draw a line down the middle.

• Down the left side, as quickly as possible, write down all the recurring thoughts that come up when you think about your problem (for example: *I'll never paint again; I have no talent; Where am I going to go from here?; I don't know what to do;* and so forth).

• Consider each of these statements in turn. Say it over and over to yourself. What feelings occur with each of the statements? Anger? Fear? Nervousness? Guilt? Shame?

• Do these statements remind you of anything anyone has ever said to you before? If so, note that person's name or that time in your life beside the statement.

• Are they things you have said to yourself at other times in your life? If so, make a note beside the feeling.

• Now, put the paper aside, make sure your dream journal is beside your bed, and write in it your problem in the form of a question. For example, if you are feeling blocked, you might write, "Why am I feeling blocked?" or "What can I do to get through this block?" If you have lost the direction of your work, you could ask, "Where should I go from here?"

• Make sure your mind is quiet and focused. Close your eyes, and imagine the gatekeeper or another helpful figure who has appeared in your dreams. See this figure in as much detail as possible. You might want to create an image of him or her in the clearing of the forest, smiling at you, and waiting for you to speak. When you have a clear image, thank the other for coming and state your question, asking him or her to provide the answer in a dream tonight. Thank him or her for listening, and open your eyes again.

• Read your question over several times just before falling asleep.

• Sleep!

• In the morning, immediately upon waking, write down your dream. Begin by writing down what thoughts, feelings, and memories each of the key elements in the dream evokes in you. This can take some time, especially with a long dream.

• If your problem involves being stuck and not knowing which way to proceed, observe the ways in which you moved within the dream, the strategies you used, and the effectiveness of those strategies (refer to chapter 8). If you have been feeling blocked, pay particular attention to your feelings within the dream and the situations in which those feelings occur (see chapter 2 and part III). Follow the thread of feeling throughout the dream to discover what emotions you may need to explore in your waking life.

• Responses to questions in dreams use the dream language. It is up to you to find the jewel within the dream.

If you are still puzzled, you may wish to visit the forest again. This time, explain to your helpful character that you were confused by the dream, and ask him or her to clarify the message. (For a more in-depth introduction to using this dialoguing technique called *active imagination,* see Robert Johnson's helpful book, *Inner Work* [HarperSanFrancisco].)

□ ～ □ ～ □ ～ □ ～ □ ～ □ ～ □ ～ □ ～ □ ～ □

Outer Creative Communities: Bringing Your Forest Journey into the World

Never doubt that a small group of commonly minded individuals can change the world. Indeed, it is the only thing that ever has.
—*Margaret Mead*

Opening yourself to your imagination and the inner figures you find there is very important. But humans are social creatures. The amount and quality of social support available to us from the outside world is positively correlated with maintaining our health, and recovering from physical and mental illness. It is one of the most important methods we have for successfully coping with stress.

Unfortunately, although having a sense of belonging is so important to all of us, it seems increasingly hard to find. It is even more difficult for people who create to feel that they are part of a community because of their strong desire for independence and feelings of differentness from other people. As we saw in chapter 3, many people who create prefer their own company and find their original expression in their silence. Nevertheless, we all do need the support, encouragement, exchange of ideas, and companionship that community brings. Being part of a group of creative friends (no matter how small) who can inspire, exhilarate, support, aid, and encourage each other will enrich our creative lives and help us become more productive.

A *community* is a group of people who share something in common that separates them from the larger society. There are all kinds of communities, and members of a community may not all know each other. Some examples of communities to which you may belong are: families; neighborhoods; high school graduates; friends, men or women; bridge players; (single) mothers or fathers; your profession; Americans or Europeans; people who live in the Southern Hemisphere; and so on.

Most people belong to a lot of communities, although we rarely pause to identify them, as we do in the following exercise. But communities are crucial. They make us feel less alone by showing us to whom we are really connected.

◻ ∼ ◻ ∼ ◻ ∼ ◻ ∼ ◻ ∼ ◻ ∼ ◻ ∼ ◻ ∼ ◻ ∼ ◻

Exercise: Your Community Map

For this exercise, you will need a large sheet of paper (the bigger, the better), several colors of pens or pencils, and about half an hour.[105]

- First, put your name in the center and surround it with a circle. Next, on a separate sheet of paper, write the names of your family members (if living) and your closest friends (including any romantic partners). Remember your inner figures!

• Think about all of these people, and consider how close you now feel to each of them. On your map, distance will represent emotional distance. Place the person's name you feel the least close to about halfway between your name and any edge of the paper. Write the name of the person you feel closest to very near your own, but still separated by a bit of space. Then, write in the names of the others at the appropriate distance between the closest and least closest person's names. You will be writing names all around your own, not in a line. Make sure you write all the names between the closest person's name and the least close person's name.

• Now, go back to your separate sheet of paper and write down all those people with whom you come in contact on a regular basis, through work, in the neighborhood, at the café—anyone you see regularly but who is not already on your map. You may wish to write down the names of groups of people (for example, bridge club, Internet newsgroup, other employees) rather than individual names at this stage. Again, consider how close you feel to that person (or group), or how important that person (or group) is to your daily life. Although you may not know the coffee shop worker very well, you may enjoy his manner, banter, and familiarity. On your map, write in the name of the person from this new list that you feel is least important to you an inch or so from the edge of the paper, and the person most important of these a bit outward from the least close person from the previous list. Fill in the other names in their appropriate places.

• Next, return to your separate sheet of paper, and jot down all the names of people who are not regularly a part of your life and are not friends or family, but are nevertheless important to you. These might be prominent people you admire, people who have died, public figures, and so on. Repeat the steps you took previously, this time skirting the edge of the paper with the names. You now have a "closeness" map of all of the people who are in your life. Draw a tight circle around each of the entries, whether they are individuals or groups.

• Take some time for reflection. How do you feel about the number of names on your map? Are there more or fewer than you thought? How many people in your life are close to you?

• Assemble your colored pens or pencils. Now, draw a line between each circled entry whose members are acquainted with members of another circled entry. (You are connected with all of these people, so you, of course, need no lines moving outward from yourself!) Begin from the circles containing your family and friends. Change colors whenever you move outward to your acquaintances and again when you reach those on the periphery of your life.

• Each of the groups of circles you have connected represents one of your communities. Mark each circle or group of linked circles that supports your creativity with a symbol that is meaningful to you (a green jewel, perhaps?). That is where you can turn for creative nourishment. Mark each circle or group of circles that sabotages your creativity (why are you associating with these people?) with another symbol (a skull and crossbones?). Those people should be avoided, especially when you are feeling insecure or blocked. Changing whom we associate with on a regular basis can completely alter our relationship with our creativity.

Nourishing Your Community

If you would like to increase your sense of community, consider how you might introduce members of some groups (or those who stand alone) to other groups. Also ponder ways of increasing your contact with those who nourish your work. Most important, come up with some things you can do to support others who create on your map, and then make sure you follow through and do them. Support begets support, and we need all we can get!

To add new people to your map, you will need to meet some. People who are creative and people who are interested in dreams are two groups guaranteed to share something in common with you. You might consider joining a local artists' or writers' group, where you will certainly meet people with similar interests who will respect and value your creativity. Attending classes or seminars for people in your creative field gives you an opportunity to strike up an opening conversation, and keeps you both stimulated and current with the happenings in your field. There are a number of group travel opportunities for creative people (particularly artists, business people, and writers), which afford you the chance to develop deeper friendships over time while learning new things and sharing your own experiences. Dream groups are offered in many towns. If there are none available where you live, consider starting your own! People who are interested in their dreams, whether or not they are creative, tend to be oriented toward inner experience and probably have something in common with you. Be diligent and persevere. Enhancing your community takes time. Add to your community map every so often; watch it change and grow as you do.

◇ ≈ ◇ ≈ ◇

Now, as we approach the end of our journey, we return to creative dreams. In this next exercise, we apply what we have learned throughout this book, as we did with Giselle's dreams, to a short dream series. This will prepare us to search through our own dream series to find our personal and unique creative jewel.

Exercise: Blanche's Dreams

Blanche is a very creative poet and writer. Here are her dreams:

> DREAM ONE: I am going for a walk by the sea, or swimming in the sea. I am swimming, walking off to the right of shore; it gets dark and the waves are getting very high. I stop at this place on shore and this man arrives who has just saved someone from drowning. He tells me I can't go back the way I came now because the water's too high and I should wait until 11:00. I tell him my daughter is waiting for me at home, would he call her when he gets to a phone and tell her I've been delayed? He says he will and takes my number.

> DREAM TWO: I'm in a library and have some books under my arm that I had checked out and was going to take home. One book is a children's book and has lots of animal pictures and rhymes about animals in it. A woman is also there with her little girl; when I'm reading this book the little girl comes over and looks at it with me; her mother says that she has a book similar to this at home. For some reason, one of the verses calls to mind a poem that starts, "If night takes the form of a whale," and this all has something to do with a class on creativity.

> DREAM THREE: I'm running by the ocean with my daughter. There are these sort of barrier reefs. Well, now that I think of it, I don't really know what a barrier reef is, but something to keep the waves steady beyond

a certain point. There's some issue about whether or not we have our shoes on. I remember running very fast and feeling really good—also, at some point, Rachel and I both run out along the reef and then the water is very high. I'm holding on to her so that it won't carry her away.

DREAM FOUR: I am in this royal castle, which seems just like a house, I think, except there's this area in the center that's sacred or something. There's a young boy here who, it turns out, is the son of a Russian czar, and there's some discussion of whether and how he will ascend to the throne. I believe I am his teacher in this dream and we do several mock sword fights. I am very conscious of this sacred space in the center and the fight seems to have something to do with it. I don't have a sword and make do with a saw.

Make three copies of the following worksheet and complete one for each of Blanche's dreams as you did with Giselle's single dream.

WORKSHEET: BLANCHE'S DREAM SERIES

ELEMENTS	PHRASES
Emotions	
Earth, Air, Fire, Water	
Children	
Loss	
Illness, Physical Problems	
Natural Obstacles	
Endangered Others	
Animals	
Threatening Others	
Helpful Shadow or Anima and Animus Figures	
Mandalas	

Now, write down what you discovered about Blanche's dream themes. Try to identify Blanche's creative jewel—that which her dreams suggest she most needs in order to enhance and express her creativity.

As we have seen in this book, emotions hold the key to dream meaning, and unexpressed emotions are often at the heart of creative blocks. Strong emotions may arise when we explore our pasts, when glimpsing shadow qualities, and when making contact with the anima or animus. Our jewel often represents those feelings and inner qualities of which we have not been aware, combined with the commitment to express them creatively. Meeting inner figures and consciously transforming them in our creative work forges the creative gem.

☐ ∿ ☐ ∿ ☐ ∿ ☐ ∿ ☐ ∿ ☐ ∿ ☐ ∿ ☐ ∿ ☐ ∿ ☐

Exercise: Finding the Jewel in Our Dreams

Those of us who are competitive and enjoy a challenge might have found ourselves analyzing our progress through this book, hoping we would soon reach the most developed stage of awareness. Really, there is no such place! It would be unwise to consider your dream life as something you progress through from start to finish. Nor are the stages of shadow or anima/animus you find in your dreams linear. Rather, as you work through your dreams, they spiral, returning again and again to the same themes, each time garnering for you more awareness and creative development. As you grow stronger, you are rewarded with increased self-insight, but you never reach the end of your creative growth.

We also typically become aware of more than just one quality about ourselves and our lives at a time, and the stages and themes in dreams reflect that fact by overlapping with one another. On average, we can find between two and three distinct, main dream themes in any series of twenty-five consecutive dreams. Such is the case with all those whose dreams enrich *The Creative Dreamer*. Because dream patterns can emerge sporadically throughout a series, it may be easier to identify recurring themes in other's dreams (like Blanche's) than in one's own dreams. The following exercise will help.

Set aside an afternoon or evening when you will be free from interruptions. Prepare for this exercise by making a copy of your dream journal. Number each dream. Search around for pens with different colored inks or erasable colored pencils. Cut the copy of your dream journal apart and tape the pieces together, if necessary, so that you have a pile of dreams, one to a sheet.

Assign a different color to each of the following themes:

> Emotions
>
> Earth, air, fire, water
>
> Children
>
> Loss
>
> Illness, physical problems
>
> Natural obstacles
>
> Animals
>
> Endangered others
>
> Threatening others
>
> Shadow/anima/animus figures
>
> Mandalas

Now, using the colored pencil for "emotions," underline the portion of each dream where emotion is mentioned, or where it is curiously absent. Continue on that way through all of the elements. You will find that more than one color will usually appear on each dream. Go through the themes one at a time, writing down the numbers of the dreams that contain that theme. For "emotions," for example, you may have dreams 1, 4, 9, and 11. Pull those dreams out, and read through them carefully, referring to chapter 2 as necessary. What emotion or emotions appear most and least frequently? Makes notes, for this exercise will give you a great deal of information about your dream life and how it relates to your creative process. For the four elements, again determine which is the most frequent, referring to chapter 8 when needed. Move through each of the themes in turn until you have explored each of them in your own dream series. When you reach "animals" and subsequent themes, watch for development and sameness across different characters in different dreams. Although they may appear in different guises, these characters might be representing the same aspect of your psyche.

Finally, write yourself a little summary of what you have discovered. As you did for Blanche, search through your series for your own green gem, your creative-block antidote. If you have trouble finding it, ask the gatekeeper or another helpful figure for guidance.

Keep your notes in a safe place. Perform this exercise every so often to map the changes in your dreaming landscape. You will find some themes evolving quickly and some more slowly. As long as you continue to give them attention, your dreams will aid you on your creative path.

Looking Back and Stepping Forward

Now is the time for endings. We have traveled long and soon will arrive where we began. I hope that *The Creative Dreamer* has been a fit companion for you on your path, and will continue to help you find what you seek. Most of all, honor what lives within you by expressing it with joy. May you travel softly and be gentle with yourself.

Please share with me your responses, thoughts, and ideas; your dreams; favorite quotations; or anything else that comes to mind. I enjoy receiving mail and I will respond. To be placed on my mailing list to receive free tips on how to increase your dream recall and information about upcoming workshops in the United States and abroad, dream and creativity groups, and creative dream journeys to faraway places, please email drtonay@veronicatonay.com or write:

Veronica Tonay, Ph.D.
P.O. Box 568
Santa Cruz, CA 95061

My website contains excerpts from my books, information on upcoming appearances, new articles on dreams, and tips and links about creativity, well-being, and dream work. Visit it at www.drtonay.com.

◻ ∼∼ ◻ ∼∼ ◻

Turning around and around, you see no clear way through the thicket, except the way you came. "Think back," says the gatekeeper, vanishing with a nod and a wink. "Follow your progress through the wood. The answer lies within the journey." You consider your travels across the meadow and into the forest where you chose your path. There, you ventured into the room of marble, and continued on to cross a bridge and fall into the river, surviving only to be confronted with a fearsome creature. Weary, you persevered through the darkest wood, faced your own reflection and, at last, reached the greatest of your trials—the gate where your insight earned you entrance to the circular clearing in which you now stand. Bewildered, you open your hand to peer carefully at the green jewel. It sparkles with the sun, and you cannot help but smile. The grass beneath you is like a ruffled, green silk spread, on which you now sit, taking off your shoes and flexing your toes. The splashing spring sends rivulets of water between them. You immerse yourself in the scents of fresh grass, pine, and clear, fresh air, and feel as though you could stay here forever. But you know this is not possible, that you have important work to do. You have something unique to bring into the world, and it will take all the strength you have gained on this journey, and on all of the journeys you have undertaken throughout your life, to accomplish it.

But what will you do, exactly? How will you bring what you have found here to the outside world? Although there is no one here with you, you hear the gatekeeper's voice resounding through the clearing: "In everything we create, we give the story of our lives. This is your own, secret place. It is a place for reviving your creative spirit and for remembering who you are and what you are to do. Take a drink of the cool spring and the way out will be revealed to you."

Shaken a bit, you do as you are bidden. Across the clearing from the place at which you entered, the air shimmers, just as it sometimes does on a ferociously hot day. Bits of light explode within the shimmering like sparklers. Popping and fizzing noises mingle with bird cries. Suddenly, an ancient portal appears. It is an arch, something like the one that marked the entrance to the forest, except this one has a great, wooden door with mysterious symbols. These are familiar to you, and you realize all at once they are the reverse of the letters of your name, carved into the other side of the door. You run to the wondrous apparition, which shimmers less and less with each step, and run your hand over the letters, satisfied. Your hand comes away fragrant with the scent of damp wood. When you pull the ornate handle, dimpled with small indentations, you discover the door is quite heavy, and you cannot open it alone.

A chorus of voices from the other side of the door sing out, "The gem! The jewel!" Ah! You open your hand again and the gem leaps out, landing in an indention just its size. The door springs open! Hesitating, you turn back toward the clearing and the forest beyond, sad to be leaving. From the center, the gatekeeper waves to you and gestures for you to go forth. Just then, the gem pops out on the other side. As you step through and the door closes, the gatekeeper's voice fades behind you: "Use the gem to return whenever you find the need."

Stunned, you find yourself by the pond, very near the circus tents where you began your journey. The others are dancing and singing, playing instruments and laughing as they welcome you home. You hide the jewel beneath a particularly luminescent rock by the pond's edge. Whenever you need to, whenever you feel stuck or blocked or lost, you can find this place again simply by envisioning the gem. When you reclaim it from its hiding place, the door to the clearing will appear.

Feeling a bit taller somehow, you turn toward the group. Your own home waits for you, with something warm to drink and your latest work ready to be created. Exhilarated, you return to the world. The words of the gatekeeper drift with laughter across the meadow, fragrant with wildflowers. The only way out is always through.

You smile and dive into the pond. . .

Notes

1   Hall, C.S., and R.L. Van de Castle. *The Content Analysis of Dreams.* New York: Meredith Publishing Co., 1966.

2   O'Shaughnessy, A. First lines from "Ode." In W.A. Perry (ed.), *Poems of Arthur O'Shaughnessy.* New Haven: Yale University Press, 1923.

3   The names and identifying characters of all dreamers, and the names and identifying characteristics in their dreams, have been changed to preserve anonymity.

4   Schneider, D.D., and L. Sharp. "The Dream Life of a Primitive People: The Dreams of the Yir Yoront of Australia." *Anthropological Studies 1.* Washington, DC: American Anthropological Association, 1969.

5   For a comprehensive and enlightening review of dream research (including cross-cultural studies on dreaming), see G.W. Domhoff *Finding Meaning in Dreams: A Quantitative Approach,* New York: Plenum, 1996.

6   The charts in this section were developed using findings from those studies on cross-cultural gender differences in dream content surveyed in G. W. Domhoff; C.N. Winget and M. Kramer, *Dimensions of Dreams,* Gainesville, Fla.: University Press, 1979; and R. L. Van de Castle, *Finding Meaning in Dreams,* 1996, *Our Dreaming Mind,* New York: Ballantine, 1994. My own studies have also replicated these findings. The following sources report on gender differences in dream content within the U.S.: C. S. Hall and G. W. Domhoff, "A Ubiquitous Sex Difference in Dreams," *Journal of Abnormal and Social Psychology*, 9, 259–267, 1963; C.S. Hall and R. L. Van de Castle, *The Content Analysis of Dreams;* and G.W. Domhoff, *Finding Meaning in Dreams.*

7   Tonay, V. K. "California Women and Their Dreams: A Historical and Sub-Cultural Comparison of Dream Content." *Journal of Imagination, Cognition, and Personality,* 10(1), 85–99, 1990.

8   Tonay, V. K. *Behavioral Continuity and Affective Compensation: The Relationship Between Dream Content and Personality.* Unpublished master's thesis, University of California at Berkeley, 1988.

9   Ruskin, J. *The Diaries of John Ruskin.* J. Evans and J.H. Whitehouse (eds.). Oxford: Clarendon Pres, 1956.

10   Lawrence, D. H. "Letter to Katherine Mansfield (dated March, 1919)." *The Collected Letters of D. H. Lawrence.* Intro. and ed. by Harry Moore. New York: Viking Penguin, 1932. Copyright 1962 by Angelo Ravagli and C. Montague Weekley, Executors of the Estate of Frieda Lawrence Ravagli. Used by permission of Viking Penguin, a division of Penguin Books, USA, Inc.

11   Sendak, M. In N. Epel (ed.), *Writers Dreaming.* New York: Vintage, 1993. Reprinted by permission of Random House, Inc.

12   Nashe, T. "The Terrors of the Night." In R.B. McKerrow (ed.), *Works.* London: Sidgwick & Jackson, 1910. (Original work published 1594.)

13   Bosnak, R. *A Little Course in Dreams.* Boston: Shambhala, 1986.

14   This list draws on findings in V. K. Tonay, *Behavioral Continuity and Affective Compensation;* A. B. Seigel, *Dreams That Can Change Your Life: Navigating Life's Passages through Turning-Point Dreams,* Los Angeles: J. P. Tarcher, 1990; and V. in F.X. Barron (Chair), *Earthquake, Selfquake: What's a Psychological to Do?,* symposium conducted at the 98th annual meeting of the American Psychological Association, Boston, 1990.

15   Nashe, T. "The Terrors of the Night."

16   Tan, A. In N. Epel (ed.), *Writers Dreaming.* Paraphrased by permission.

17   Nichols, J. Ibid.

18   Gibbs, R.W., Jr. *The Poetics of Mind: Figurative Thought, Language, and Understanding.* Cambridge, England: Cambridge University Press, 1994.

19   Lakoff, G. *Women, Fire, and Dangerous Things: What Categories Reveal about the Mind.* Chicago: University of Chicago Press, 1987.

20   Gibbs, R.W., Jr. *The Poetics of Mind.*

21   Gedo, M. M. *Picasso: Art as Autobiography.* Chicago: University of Chicago Press, 1980.

22   Chart adapted from content analysis scoring instructions for emotion, presented in C. S. Hall and R. L. Van de Castle, *The Content Analysis of Dreams,* 110–14, and reprinted in G.W. Domhoff, *Finding Meaning in Dreams.*

23 Normative values from C. S. Hall and R. L. Van de Castle, *The Content Analysis of Dreams,* 110–14.

24 Normative values here and in the remainder of the chapter are from G. W. Domhoff, *Finding Meaning in Dreams,* and C. S. Hall and R. L. Van de Castle, *The Content Analysis of Dreams.* Normative values and findings on the relationship between creativity and dreams, here and in the remainder of the chapter are from the following sources:
 G. Domino, "Primary Process Thinking in Dream Reports as Related to Creative Achievement", *Journal of General Psychology,* 99(2), 929–932, 1976; W. H. Sylvia, P. M. Clark, and L. J. Monroe, "Dream Reports of Subjects High and Low in Creative Ability," *Journal of General Psychology,* 99(2), 205–211, 1978; V. K. Tonay, *Behavioral Continuity and Affective Compensation,* V. K. Tonay, "Dreams, Creativity, and Personal Adjustment," paper presented at the 98th annual meeting of the American Psychological Association, Boston, 1990; V. K. Tonay, *Creativity and Dreaming,* Dissertation Abstracts International, 1993; and J. M. Wood, D. Sebba, and G. Domino, "Do Creative People Have More Bizarre Dreams? A Reconsideration," *The Journal of Imagination, Cognition, and Personality,* 9(1), 3–16.

25 Coleridge, S.T. *Notebooks.* K. Coburn (ed.). New York: Pantheon Books, 1957.

26 Coleridge, S.T. From a letter to Robert Southey, dated September 1803.

27 Angelou, M. In N. Epel (ed.), *Writers Dreaming.* Reprinted by permission.

28 Introductory books on basic Freudian and Jungian psychological theory are: A. Storr, *Freud,* Oxford: Oxford University Press, 1989; and A. Storr, *Jung,* New York: Routledge, 1991. Several fine books on dreams outline the classical dream theories of Freud and Jung. Among them are: S. Freud, *The Interpretation of Dreams,* New York: Basic Books, 1953; S. Freud, *On Dreams,* New York: Norton, 1952; C. G. Jung, *Dreams,* R. F. C. Hull (trans.), Princeton: Princeton University Press, 1974; C. G. Jung, *The Collected Works of C.G. Jung,* H. Read (ed.), Princeton: Princeton University Press, 1974 (writings directly related

to dreams include vol. 4, *The Analysis of Dreams,* and vol. 8, *General Aspects of Dream Psychology)*; G.G. Globus, *Dream Life, Wake Life: The Human Condition through Dreams,* Albany, N.Y.: State University of New York Press, 1987; A. Moffit, M. Kramer, and R. Hoffman (eds.), *The Functions of Dreaming,* Albany, N.Y.: State University of New York Press, 1993; and R. L. Van de Castle, *Our Dreaming Mind,* New York: Ballantine, 1994.

29   Studies on dream recall and frequency include: Kerr, N.H. "Mental Imagery, Dreams, and Perception," in C. Cavallero and D. Foulkes (eds.), *Dreaming as Cognition,* 18–37, London: Harvester Wheatsheaf, 1993; M. Schredl, "Creativity and Dream Recall," *Journal of Creative Behavior,* 29, 16–24, 1995; N. P. Spanos, J. S. Henderikus, H. L. Ratke, and M. E. Nightingale, "Absorption in Imaginings, Sex-Role Orientation, and the Recall of Dreams by Males and Females," *Journal of Personality Assessment,* 44(3), 277–282, 1980; and V. K. Tonay, "Personality Correlates of Dream Recall: Who Remembers?" *Dreaming,* 3(1), 1–7, 1993.

30   Whitman, W. *Washington Star.* November 16, 1875.

31   Greene, G. *A World of My Own: A Dream Diary.* New York: Penguin, 1994.

32   Mistral, F. *Memories of Mistral.* C. E. Maud (trans.). London: E. Arnold, 1907.

33   Tonay, V. K. *Creativity and Dreaming.*

34   A review of the IPAR studies whose findings are conveyed throughout this chapter can be found in the following five sources: F. X. Barron, *Creativity and Psychological Health,* Buffalo: The Creative Education Foundation, 1990; R. Helson, "Women Mathematicians and the Creative Personality," *Journal of Consulting and Clinical Psychology,* 36, 210–211, 217–220, 1971; Institute of Personality Assessment and Research, University of California, Berkeley, *The Creative Person,* Berkeley: University Extension, 1961; and D. W. MacKinnon, "Genus Architectus Creator Varietas Americanus," *American Institute of Architects Journal,* 31–35, September 1960; and D. W. MacKinnon, "Personality and the Realization of Creative Potential," *American Psychologist,* 29, 273–281, 1965.

35   Albert, R.S., "Observations and Suggestions Regarding Giftedness, Familial Influence, and the Attainment of Eminence," *Gifted Child Quarterly,* 22, 201–211, 1978; A. Roe, "A Psychological Study of Eminent Psychologists and Anthropologists, and a Comparison with Biological and Physical Scientists," *Psychological Monographs: General and Applied,* 67, 1953; and D.K. Simonton, *Genius, Creativity, and Leadership: Historiometric Inquiries,* Cambridge, Mass.: Harvard University Press, 1984.

36   Goertzel, M. G., V. Goertzel, and T. G. Goertzel. *Three Hundred Eminent Personalities.* San Francisco: Jossey-Bass, 1978.

37   Berry, C. "The Nobel Scientists and the Origins of Scientific Achievement." *British Journal of Sociology,* 32, 381–391, 1981.

38   Vidal, G. *Matters of Fact and Fiction.* London: Heinemann, 1977.

39   Eisenstadt, J. M. "Parental Loss and Genius." *American Psychologist,* 33, 211–223, 1978.

40   Albert, R.S. "Family Positions and the Attainment of Eminence: A Study of Special Family Positions and Special Family Experiences." *Gifted Child Quarterly,* 22, 201–211, 1980.

41   Ochse, R. *Before the Gates of Excellence.*

42   Ibid.

43   Goertzel, V., and M.G. Goertzel. *Cradles of Eminence.* London: Constable, 1962.

44   Adler, A. *The Individual Psychology of Alfred Adler: A Systematic Presentation of Selections from His Writings.* H.L. and R.R. Ansbacher (eds.). New York: Basic Books, 1956.

45   Sendak, M. In N. Epel, (ed.), *Writers Dreaming.* Reprinted by permission.

46   Terman, L. M., and M. H. Oden, *The Gifted Child Grows Up: Twenty-five Years' Follow-up of the Superior Child* (vol. 4 of L. M. Therman, *Genetic Studies of Genius*), Palo Alto, Calif.: Stanford University Press, 1959; C. M. Cox, *The Early Mental Traits of Three Hundred Geniuses* (vol. 2 of L. M. Terman, *Genetic Studies of Genius*), Palo Alto, Calif.: Stanford University Press, 1926; and F. Galton, *Hereditary Genius,* New York: Appleton, 1869.

47 Mozart, W. A. Quoted in J. Ehrenwald, *Anatomy of Genius: Split Brains and Global Minds.* New York: Human Sciences Press, 1984.

48 Barron, F. X. *Creativity and Personal Freedom.* Princeton: Van Nostrand, 1968.

49 Barron, Ibid.; and R. B. Cattell, *Abilities and Their Structure, Growth, and Action,* Boston: Houghton Mifflin, 1971. For excellent discussions of these studies, and, more generally, the relationship between creativity and psychopathology, see R. Ochse, *Before the Gates of Excellence,* and A. Storr, *The Dynamics of Creation,* New York: Ballantine, 1993.

50 Karlsson, J.L. "Genetic Association of Giftedness and Creativity with Schizophrenia." *Hereditas,* 66, 177–182, 1970.

51 King, S. In N. Epel (ed.), *Writers Dreaming.* Reprinted by permission.

52 Ochse, R. *Before the Gates of Excellence.*

53 Frost, R. "The Road Not Taken." In E.C. Lathem (ed.), *The Poetry of Robert Frost.* Copyright 1944 by Robert Frost. Copyright 1916, 1969 by Henry Holt & Co., Inc. Reprinted by permission of Henry Holt & Co., Inc.

54 Angelou, M. In N. Epel (ed), *Writers Dreaming.* Reprinted by permission.

55 Information in parts II and III on the relationship between dream themes and creativity is taken from: V. K. Tonay, "Dream Themes of Subjects High and Low in Creativity," paper presented at the 102nd annual meeting of the American Psychological Association, Los Angeles, California, August 1994; and V. K. Tonay, *Dream Themes of Those High and Low in Creativity,* ms. in preparation. A creatively written, well-researched reference for the interpretation of general dream themes is D. Fontana, *The Secret Language of Dreams,* San Francisco: Chronicle Books, 1994.

56 Ernst, M. In B. Ghiselin (ed.), *The Creative Process.* New York: Mentor, 1950.

57 The following are among those who have advanced biologically based, cognitive theories of dreaming, relating the brain activity during sleep that produces dreams to the processes of waking creative thought: J.A. Hobson, *The Dreaming Brain,* New York: Basic Books, 1988; H. Hunt, *The Multiplicity of Dreams: A Cognitive Psychological Perspective,* New Haven:

Yale University Press, 1989; H. Krystal and A. Krystal, "Psychoanalysis and Neuroscience in Relationship to Dreams and Creativity," in M. P. Shaw and M. A. Runco (eds.), *Creativity and Affect: Creativity Research,* 185–212, Norwood, New Jersey: Ablex, 1994; and J. Winson, *Brain and Psyche: The Biology of the Unconscious,* New York: Anchor Press, 1995.

58 Freud, S., *The Interpretation of Dreams,* and S. R. Palombo, "The Genius of the Dream," *American Journal of Psychoanalysis,* 43(4), 301–313, 1983.

59 See chapters 9 and 10 on anima figures in dreams.

60 Domino, G., "Primary Process Thinking in Dream Reports as Related to Creative Achievement," *Journal of Consulting and Clinical Psychology,* 44, 929–932, 1976; and J. M. Wood, D. Sebba, and G. Domino, "Do Creative People Have More Bizarre Dreams?"

61 Stevenson, R.L. *A Chapter on Dreams.* 1892.

62 Shelley, M. *Frankenstein, or the Modern Prometheus* (Introduction). London: H. Colburn and R. Bentley, 1831.

63 Gilchhrist, A. *The Life of William Blake.* London: John Lane Co., 1907.

64 Allende, I. In N. Epel (ed.), *Writers Dreaming.* Paraphrased by permission.

65 Wellesley, D. Letter from Dorothy Wellesley to W. B. Yeats, dated 12 November, 1936. *Letters on Poetry from W. B. Yeats to Dorothy Wellesley.* London: Oxford University Press, 1964. Reprinted by permission of Oxford University Press.

66 Yeats, W.B. Ibid.

67 The Association for the Study of Dreams is a nonprofit organization; anyone interested in dreams can join. For more information, write to the ASD, P.O. Box 1600, Vienna, VA 22183.

68 Wellesley, D. *Letters on Poetry from W. B. Yeats to Dorothy Wellesley.* Reprinted by permission of Oxford University Press.

69 Jung, C. G. *Dreams.*

70 Huntington, L. "An Inkwell of the Unconscious." *Psychological Perspectives,* 17(1), 111–124, 1986.

71 von Franz, M.-L. *Puer Aeturnus,* Sigo Press, 1970; M. -L. von Franz, "The Ladder to Heaven," In F. Boa (ed.), *The Way of the Dream,* Toronto: Windrose Films, 1988.

72 Cuddy, M., and K. Belicki. "Nightmare Frequency and Related Sleep Disturbances as a History of Sexual abuse." *Dreaming,* 2(1), 15–22, 1992. V. K. Tonay. "Holding Back the Night: The Dreams of Women Sexually Abused as Children." Paper presented as part of the symposium *Women's Bodies, Women's Dreams* at the 5th annual conference of the ASD, June, 1988. (Summarized in *Psychology Today,* March 1988.)

73 Tolstoy, L. *Anna Karenina.* N.H. Dole (trans.), New York: Crowell, 1886.

74 Van de Castle, R. L. *Our Dreaming Minds.*

75 Hall, C. S. *The Individual and His Dreams.*

76 A resource for learning about this dialoguing technique, called active imagination, is R. Johnson's *Inner Work,* New York: Harper & Row, 1986.

77 For a collection of articles relating to the psychological significance of the four elements, see the Spring 1995 issue of *Parabola.*

78 King, S. In N. Epel (ed.), *Writers Dreaming.* Reprinted by permission.

79 Chetwynd, T. *A Dictionary of Symbols.* London: Paladin, 1982.

80 Estés, C.P. *Women Who Run with the Wolves: Myths and Stories of the Wild Woman Archetype.* New York: Ballantine, 1992.

81 Dante. *The Inferno of Dante.* R. Pinsky (trans.). New York: Farrar, Straus & Giroux, 1994. Reprinted by permission.

82 For Carl Jung's writings on the shadow archetype, see Jung, C. G., *The Archetypes and the Collective Unconscious.* New York: Bollingen Foundation, 1959.

83 Chetwynd, T. *A Dictionary of Symbols.*

84 Ibid.

85 Rilke, R.M. *Letters to a Young Poet.* M. D. H. Norton (trans.). New York: W. W. Norton & Co, Inc., 1934.

86 For writings on the anima/animus archetype, see Jung, E., *Anima and Animus,* Dallas: Spring Pubs., 1957. For more on the relationship between women's dreams and the animus, see Scott, S., "Dreams and Creativity in Women," *Arts and Psychotherapy,* 14(4), 293–299, 1987.

87 The table was compiled with information from C.G. Jung, *The Archetypes and the Collective Unconscious,* E. Jung, *Anima and Animus,* and M. -L. von Frantz, "The Psychology of Women."

88 For a referral to a psychologist in your area, check the Yellow Pages listings under "psychologist." For information on how to choose a psychologist, call the American Psychological Association at (202) 336-5700 and request a copy of the free brochure on how to select a psychologist.

89 Allende, I. In N. Epel (ed.), *Writers Dreaming.* Paraphrased by permission.

90 Neumann, E. *The Great Mother: An Analysis of the Archetype.* R. Manheim (trans.). New York: Pantheon, 1970.

91 von Franz, M. -L. "The Psychology of Women," 214–215.

92 Ibid.

93 Hall, C. S., and R. L. Van de Castle. *The Content Analysis of Dreams.*

94 Domhoff, G.W. *Finding Meaning in Dreams.*

95 Freud, S. *The Interpretation of Dreams.*

96 Jung, C.G. *Dreams.*

97 Nichols, J. In N. Epel (ed.), *Writers Dreaming.* Reprinted by permission.

98 Adler, A. *The Individual Psychology of Alfred Adler.* H.L. and R.R. Ansbacher (eds.). New York: Basic Books, 1956.

99 Jung, C.G., M.-L. von Franz, J.L. Henderson, J. Jacobi, and A. Jaffe. *Man and His Symbols.* Garden City, N.Y.: Doubleday & Co., 1964.

100 Kanno, S. "Symbol as Transformation and Creation: A Point of View from Analytical Psychology." *Japanese Psychological Review,* 30(1), 112–125, 1987.

101 Jung, C.G. *Symbols of Transformation.* R.F.C. Hull (trans.). Princeton: Princeton University Press, 1956.

102 Angelou, M. In N. Epel (ed.), *Writers Dreaming.* Reprinted by permission.

103 Sendak, M. Ibid.

104 For example, H. Reed, *Dream Solutions,* San Rafael, Calif.: New World Library, 1996.

105 For this exercise, I adapted an idea originally presented in C.R. Shaffer and K. Anundsen, *Creating Community Anywhere: Finding Support and Connection in a Fragmented World,* New York: Putnam Pub. Group, 1993.

Index

Note: tables are indicated by t